MY 21 YEARS
IN THE WHITE HOUSE

ALONZO FIELDS

My 21 Years
in the White House

To my wife Edna, my daughter Virginia

and

my granddaughters Victoria and Andrea

Author's Note

I want to express my deepest appreciation to former President Harry S. Truman for the encouragement he gave me when I told him that I was going to write a book about my experiences in the White House. I did not, of course, consult Mr. Truman on anything I have written.

I am grateful to William Hillman who has been my sponsor and guide through the many intricacies of writing and publishing.

I wish, too, to acknowledge the help of Laura Lou Brookman and Peter Briggs of *The Ladies Home Journal* and of Thomas P. Coffey, my editor at Coward-McCann.

CONTENTS

Chapter 1

ALLOW ME TO INTRODUCE MYSELF

*F*or more than twenty-one years I served the White House as butler, chief butler and maître d'hôtel. Beginning in October, 1931, through February, 1953, I planned and directed all the family, state, and social functions of four Presidents and kept the inventories of china, glassware, table linens, and silverware. The famous gold service was in my trust; and believe me, no one left the pantry until each piece was accounted for after a dinner party. As the maître d'hôtel, I was further required to plan all the menus and direct the activities of the butlers and the kitchen.

In these years I came in contact with kings, queens, prime ministers, princes, princesses, generals, admirals; labor, political, race, and church leaders; and some of the rabble rousers. In this book I shall try to cite many of these men and women as they impressed me.

I will also speak of the satisfactions and advantages of my job and of the opportunities that surpassed those I might have had anywhere else in the world. I should first of all say that working in the White House was not my first dream or ambition. I had always wanted to be a concert singer and it took a lot of wrenching to get this artistic streak out of my system. As a matter of fact, I am not sure that I ever got it completely out of my system.

In a way perhaps it was the artistic viewpoint that helped me adjust to life with the Presidents. I believed that in a small way I was a part of history; I felt that I was playing some role for the man who holds the greatest job in the world. I constantly kept this thought before myself during the whole time I worked in the White House until it became almost a sense of dedication.

As I always told the Negro servants and dining room help that worked for me, "Boys, remember that we are helping to make history. We have a small part, perhaps a menial part, but they can't do much here without us. They've got to eat, you know." Some, of course, thought that this was a joke. But I still kept up my preaching.

What gave me the greatest satisfaction during my years in the White House was the opportunity to observe people, the most influential people in the world in our time. I've always been interested in looking at people and studying them to see why they are different. I know that many people are cynical about our leaders and think they are all out for themselves, but I've seen the sacrifices that these leaders make. This confirmed me in my belief that the greatest value in life is really sacrifice—sacrifice for what we believe is right and for what will help the people of the world.

Perhaps the most important advantage of working in the White House was that I felt more attached to my country, got to know it and love it better, and acquired a sense of its destiny. After a while I was able to feel that destiny at work among the nations of the world. My pride increased daily in what a great country we have, and in its outstanding founders and leaders. As I look back over twenty-one years in the White House, I am very happy that I was able to serve at so important a place in so critical a period in our history. Just think what a time it was and what a privilege it was for me to watch some of the most important men and events at such an intimate range.

Chapter 2

HOW I GOT IN THE WHITE HOUSE

*H*ow did I get this position? Did I prepare and plan for such a career? No, I did not plan, nor had I ever entertained the least thought of being so close to the great men and women of this era.

How I got my job in the White House is a long and involved story—and one that led not through the front but the *back* door of the great building in which I spent the best part of my life. I was born in Lyles, in Gibson County, Indiana, which is about five miles from Princeton, the county seat, and about one hundred and twenty miles east of St. Louis. Lyles was an all-colored community with a post office, general store, church, picnic grounds, school and a baseball diamond. The trains between Louisville and St. Louis could be flagged down twice a day, for Lyles was a center for farmers to ship corn, wheat, stock and food produce.

My father kept the general store and ran an agency for the flour mills at Princeton. Dad was born in Spencer County, Kentucky, near Owensboro. He was a farm boy and lived on the farm until his family moved to Indiana. In Indiana he worked on the family farm then opened a business in groceries which later became the general store, and finally went to Washington on a political appointment in the Post Office Department, where he was a custodian. My mother kept a boardinghouse for the railroad section hands. She was born in Indiana on the farm through which her great-grandfather had given the railroad company the right of way on condition that the community would benefit by having the east- and west bound trains stop there twice a day.

Father was the organizer and director of the only military-trained, colored brass band in the southern part of Indiana. Brass bands were popular in those days for Sunday-afternoon concerts, picnics, and parades.

The general store was the center of activities. In the summer there were band practice and drilling once a week, horseshoe pitching and tall tales by rail road section hands and farm hands. In the long winter nights there were always band practice, politics, checkers, and still taller tales, mostly about hunting and the wisdom of some old hound dog. Some of the older men had been slaves and served in the Civil War, and some of the younger men had been in the Spanish-American War. A youngster, listening, would not want to go to bed.

One of the men had been a sergeant in the Negro cavalry which charged up San Juan Hill in Cuba to help Teddy Roosevelt and his Roughriders out of a tight spot. He never related much about the actual fighting, but the meeting of Teddy Roosevelt he never stopped talking about. The sergeant would always finish his evening performance by saying, "Just think. He is now the President of these United States and on top of the world without any worries."

I, too, thought any man who could be President of the United States must be on top of the world. And what worries could he have? Little did I realize that twenty-three years later I would start my adventure of holding the chair of four Presidents. The President of these United States is on top of the world in a mighty powerful seat, but I learned that it can be a very hot and troublesome seat at times.

Because brass bands were so popular in our parts and because of my father's role in Lyles' band I had planned a musical career from as far back as I can remember. After we moved to Indianapolis Dad and I played in the Y. M. C. A. military brass band. In my early twenties I was teaching all the brass instruments. I had trained choirs, studied voice, and sat on panels as a judge of choir contests. Father O'Brien, of St. Rita's church, where I helped in benefits for the Holy Name Society, of which I was an honorary member, had named me the Black John McCormack and instructed me in the diction of Irish ballads. So it appeared I was "most likely to succeed" in my chosen field.

No matter how popular and respected the musical field, however, I still had to earn my living in another way. So I ran a grocery store and meat market just as my father had done. My store was in Indianapolis. Around 1925, following a business panic in that community, my store unfortunately began to fail. Returns got to be less and less, so I gave up the business completely and went to the New England Conservatory of Music in Boston to take a graduate course in public-school music. While I was there I must have impressed the faculty, because they soon suggested that I take the artist's course—a group of studies directed toward concert work.

But soon my funds ran low. A new friend, Postello Jones, said that he would speak to his boss, Dr. Samuel W. Stratton, president of Massachusetts Institute of Technology, in Cambridge, about me. Despite the fact that, other than grocery clerking and music, there was little I was qualified for, Dr. Stratton and Morris Parris, his secretary, offered to help me. If I wanted to try being a butler, Mr. Parris said he would train me.

This gentleman from an old Georgetown family of high standing knew etiquette and society backward and forward as well as I knew my chromatic scales. I confess I didn't relish the thought of being a house servant, but Mr. Parris pointed out that, if I ever did reach the heights as a concert singer, these conventions he was teaching me would give me a background of good breeding. Dr. Stratton was a connoisseur of china, silver, cut glass, crystal, and period furniture. With these surroundings and with time provided for study and permission to practice in the reception hall of the school's residence for the president, I did my best to master the job.

It was an education to know and to be able to appreciate these fine things of good living. Here I met men like Thomas Edison, Otto Kahn, Lessing Rosenwald, John D. Rockefeller, Gerard Swope, President Lowell of Harvard, and the famous lady, Hetty Green. President Lowell I remember with special fondness. He frequently visited the house of the president of M. I. T. for dinners and receptions and teas. Very often on my travels in the subway I was most surprised to see President Lowell. One day he was sitting across the train from me, recognized me and came across to sit and speak with me. We conversed for the rest of the trip.

I guess he enjoyed riding the public conveniences but in those days this was a very exceptional thing; few people of his position would dare do it because the trains of those days were not as comfortable as they are today. But President Lowell was very interested in life and people. At first I was a little hesitant to talk to the president, especially when he questioned me about the matters of the day, such as race conditions. I felt he was trying to get my opinion without really being interested in it and I hesitated in talking to him. Finally, however, I lost all fear and inhibition and felt that he was really interested in people. As a result I grew interested in him and we came to have some very serious conversations. I was often surprised to know that we were very often in agreement on how many situations should be approached.

One of the most important in landing me the job at the White House was Lieutenant Frederic Butler, long since a general. He made several trips to M. I. T. in studies of Army engineering and, being a friend of Mr. Parris, always stopped at the house.

When Dr. Stratton dropped dead while talking to a reporter about the death of Thomas Edison, Lieutenant Butler proved to be a real friend to me. At the time of Dr. Stratton's death I had an agreement with Arthur Wilson of Boston, a voice teacher of wide reputation, to prepare me for my concert debut. For one year after that he was to receive lo per cent of my earnings and for the next two years 15 percent. Tentative arrangements were made for the concert in Jordan Hall in April of 1932.

As fate would have it, a telephone call came for me from the White House. I was startled until I heard the voice of Lieutenant Butler. He was an aide to President Hoover, and Mrs. Butler was Mrs. Hoover's secretary.

I had served tea to Mrs. Hoover and her son, Mr. Allan, at Dr. Stratton's when she had visited Mr. Allan while he was at Harvard. That fleeting moment was the only time I had ever seen the First Lady. However, the lieutenant said that Mrs. Hoover felt it would be best for me to come to work at the White House, as it was likely to be a hard winter. It turned out that they could not have been more correct. I am sure there are still a few people around who remember the winter of 1931.

This was the best (and only) offer I had. So, with a wife and child depending on me, an ambitious pride to be a concert singer faded into the background. Food and shelter were the paramount issues for my family. I know I should have been elated and I knew, as most people told me, that I was lucky to have a job at the White House. But I had a premonition that this was going to be a very long winter for me and that somehow, regardless of my efforts, fate might be deciding my singing career. As you can see, my winter was twenty-one years and four months long.

I went by bus to Washington in order to save money. As I traveled through Massachusetts, Rhode Island, Connecticut, New York, New Jersey and Pennsylvania I could see idle factories and soup lines. Just to see jobless men gave me a depressed feeling and also a thankful feeling for, except for the grace of God, I, too, could be one of those wanderers. I wondered what the White House would be like.

Lieutenant Butler had told me to arrive at 10:30 at the east entrance of the White House and to ask the officer on duty for him. So at the appointed time I arrived and gave my name to the guard. I had a suitcase packed with a tuxedo and full dress, ready to go to work. Shortly Lieutenant Butler arrived and off we went through the long corridor of the ground floor, into the east wing of the house and on through the corridor of the main house, up a winding, spiral stairs to the butler's pantry.

Chapter 3

INSIDE THE WHITE HOUSE

*T*here were four or five men at work in the pantry. Lieutenant Butler inquired for Ellis. I was told that Ellis Sampson was the head man, but he wasn't in. Then Lieutenant Butler inquired for Connie. He said, "Encarnación is the second man in charge."

Encarnación was in the dining room and we went there. In the middle of the huge room I saw two men polishing a great, round mahogany table. The table was centered under a big silver chandelier with 100 or more candle bulb lights. The lieutenant introduced me to Encarnación and told him I would be working on the butler's staff. He said to me, "Connie will take care of you."

Encarnación Rodriguez was a Puerto Rican, very polite and soft-spoken. He took me back into the pantry and introduced me to the other men. I could see a puzzled expression on his face. He turned to one of the men, Robert Neal, and said, "Neal, will you show this new man the locker room?"

I was assigned a locker and I changed clothes and reported back to the pantry. When I arrived the men were all in a huddle. I could feel the conversation was about me, because upon my appearance the huddle broke up. Connie assigned me to a big tray of flat silverware and a rouge pad. I had never seen so much flatware in my life and said, "Did you have a party last night?" Connie replied, "No, just a daily routine."

After I had my lunch Mr. Neal approached Mr. Rodriguez and said, "Since Fields has his uniform, you might as well take him into the dining room tonight for dinner. As you know, Mrs. Hoover doesn't like men as tall as he is. You might as well get it over with so he can be on his way back to Boston tomorrow."

I kept my poker face and went about my assignments. At last the hour approached and I was assigned to Mrs. Hoover's side of the table. I could feel the tension and I imagined that they were anticipating Mrs. Hoover's saying, "Get that big galoot out of here."

The dining-room doors were open. Candles on the table were lit and the heavy drapes at the windows were drawn. Soon the President and the First Lady would enter through the open door. We stood in our positions near the table. My back was toward the door and, of course, I was ordered not to turn to see who was entering when the signal was received that the President was approaching.

Suddenly the quietness of the silence was broken by Mrs. Hoover's voice: "Fields, I heard that you were here. I'm so glad to see you." Mrs. Hoover went on, "Father, you remember my telling you about Fields, Dr. Stratton's man?" It was the family custom of the Hoovers to address each other as "Father" and "Mother."

The President, nodding, said, "Hello, Fields."

There was an expression of amazement on the faces of the other butlers. No one said a word when we returned to the pantry for a change of service for the next course. Well, the next day the rumors had it that I had been brought there to take over as head man. "So this is the White House," I thought. "The help gossips here just like any other place."

This White House was one busy place. Three days after my arrival I was assigned to the President's medicine-ball table, which sounds like a big promotion. It did not inflate my ego, for it meant that I had to be at work at 6:30 A.M. The President played medicine ball in the south grounds of the White House with several members of his Cabinet and one member of the Supreme Court, Justice Stone. The Cabinet members were Secretary of Interior Wilbur, Assistant Secretary of the Navy Jahncke, Secretary of War Hurley, Secretary of Commerce Chapin, Attorney General Mitchell. There were also Dr.—later Admiral—Boone, the President's personal doctor, and Secretaries Richey and Newton.

Breakfast was always served under the magnolia tree said to have been planted by President Jackson in memory of his wife, Rachel—unless it rained or after a heavy snowfall. In such cases breakfast would be in the China Room on the ground floor where the presidential china of different periods is exhibited. Serving breakfast in a jacket during the cool spring and fall mornings wasn't too pleasant, especially when just about as I started to pour a cup of coffee the weeping leaves of the magnolia would drip cold tears on the back of my neck. I had to anticipate those tears or else jump out of my skin.

The President and his ball players were wrapped up in blankets like so many Indians. Breakfast would consist of grapefruit, toast, and coffee. I never knew just how many to prepare for. I would set up for fourteen or fifteen and, as they played, count noses from a distance to see who might have come in at the last minute with a guest. One guest we always depended on was Mark Sullivan, the newspaper columnist.

There would be fifteen or twenty minutes of discussion of the happenings on The Hill, advice from the Attorney General as to the legality of certain moves, and the feel of the public by Mr. Sullivan and members of the Cabinet, as well as Justice Stone. The President seldom led in these discussions but listened and asked questions. Then he would leave after the second cup of coffee had been poured.

On leaving the table he would say to Mr. Sullivan, "Coming, Mark?" The President would go to his room and freshen up to join Mrs. Hoover for breakfast, usually in the Monroe Room on the second floor.

Breakfast was always on time at eight o'clock. In fact, the Hoovers were punctual with all meals, and each detail had to be as precise as a ritual. Luncheon was at one o'clock and dinner at eight. The Hoovers were most formal. At dinner the President always wore a dinner jacket, and all meals except breakfast were served in the State Dining Room—even the very few times when the President would dine alone. Often just the President and First Lady would dine together in this formal setting.

Dinner always consisted of seven courses—an entree, soup, fish, a meat course, salad, dessert and a serving of fruit. After each service I took my position and stood at attention. Above all, I could show no interest in the conversation. To smile at some joking remark, overheard by chance, would mean the last time I would go into the dining room. I approached the table to change services in a dignified, alive manner, but never rushing or hurried. There could be no scraping of plates. The tinkle of silver or china would invite an immediate report to the head man.

If it was a family meal the Hoovers would retire to the second floor after the fruit course for the demitasse, perhaps to the Oval Room or the West Hall. Mrs. Hoover sometimes took tea in a demitasse instead of her decaffeinated coffee, so I always had a pot of each for her.

These were the days of prohibition, and though some of the President's friends might have had some home-brew at home, it was not so with this Quaker gentleman. He disapproved of women smoking, so no smokes were served the ladies at any functions. Mrs. Hoover would politely tell ladies that the President didn't approve of women smoking.

The President was a cigar smoker. This reminds me of an incident during the serving of tea in the Green Parlor for Lady Astor and His Lordship. The President seldom attended teas. In fact, he didn't drink tea. So when we were alerted that he would be present we always prepared orangeade for him.

He arrived after the tea had been in progress for a few minutes. He greeted Lady Astor and His Lordship and apologized for being tardy. I served the orangeade to the President as usual. When he had finished he placed the glass on a little serving table and asked permission to smoke, which naturally was granted. He pulled out a cigar, took off the wrapper and tossed it into the empty glass, although an ash tray was nearby. Encarnación did not see the wrapper in the glass. He approached the President and inquired if he cared for another glass of orangeade. Before I could signal, Connie had filled the glass. The President lifted it to drink and saw the wrapper. Without hesitating, he took the wrapper out with his fingers and drank the orangeade, then placed the wrapper in the ash tray. Poor Connie nearly had a stroke. He was afraid Mrs. Hoover had seen the incident, for there was little she missed in a breach of service.

Around this time the veterans were a little restless over various grievances. Some who were called the "bonus marchers" gathered at Anacostia, Maryland, on the other side of the Potomac and planned a march on Washington. So many of them were grouped over there that General MacArthur was called to the White House to have a conference with President Hoover. MacArthur impressed me as a very stalwart man with attractive appearance. He always looked well in his uniform. He was, of course, a professional general with all the appearance of one and he seemed to enjoy it. I don't mean by that he was overbearing, or anything like that. I just mean he was very proud and very distinguished looking. Perhaps he belonged to another generation—a generation, say, with a flair of Napoleon in it. I don't know what their conversation was about but in the next few hours General MacArthur ordered the Army to block the streets. I recall the day very clearly and remember seeing the soldiers in their armored trucks driving up Pennsylvania Avenue to keep the "bonus marchers" on the other side of the river.

Chapter 4

MY FIRST STATE DINNER

$\mathcal{T}$ he first state dinner I served was given by the President in honor of the Italian Minister of Foreign Affairs, Grandi. Many people were excited over Il Duce Mussolini, Premier of Italy, and Grandi was making a state visit. The huge horseshoe table was set with the famous Monroe gold-mirrored plaque in seven sections, about twenty feet long and two and a half feet wide, with bowls of flowers reflected in the mirror. The tall gold candelabra each held a cluster of forty-four candles, and tall gold epergnes were filled with fruit, with luscious Belgian grapes in bunches draping over the sides. The gold table flat ware was laid out on the finest white damask linen. Two high-backed chairs stood at the center of the table for the President and First Lady, across from each other. Small gold chairs were placed around the inside and outside of the table, with a cluster of palms forming a background in the open space of the horse shoe.

This was the White House dining room in all its glory. There were ninety guests for the dinner. Ten services were required to serve the party, nine guests to a service and two butlers at each service. The White House was then and still is inadequate for serving a large party because of the size of the pantry. It is so designed that there isn't much that can be done about this situation.

The horseshoe type of table was built by carpenters of different-sized tables according to the requirements of the dinner party. The smallest type of table seated 65 guests and the largest size seated 104. I understand that the Eisenhowers used an E-shaped table on state occasions. We talked of such a table during the Roosevelt Administration, but that was as far as it went.

The largest table went within four feet of the walls on the outside of the horseshoe. Butlers serving on the far side of the table had to cross through the Red Room. Men serving the inside curve of the table had to enter the room first, with others following in rotation. The pantry, at that time a long narrow room with an old-fashioned manual dumb-waiter, was useless for a party. Platters of food had to be passed up a spiral stairway by a chain line of pantry crew, and some of the butlers also went down to the kitchen by the back stairs for their service. It is a wonder that the food could be kept hot.

Well, the dinner started off with a crab-meat cocktail, soup julienne, Melba toast, curled celery and olives, broiled fillet of sole with tartare sauce, sliced tomatoes and whole-wheat bread cucumber sandwiches, roast boned turkey, string beans and potatoes au gratin, green salad with Camembert cheese. For dessert there were replica ice cream molds of the White House, with the Belgian grapes served with the mints.

Then the ladies retired to the Green Room for demitasses and the gentlemen to the Red Room for demitasses and smokes. The only glasses on the table were for mineral water.

When you are invited to dine at the White House you can be certain at a state dinner that you will be at the same table with the President, even if you are perhaps fifty or ninety seats removed from him. The President is always first in the room, first to leave the table, and first to be served at all meals—even the family meals. So the butlers are always instructed to watch for the signal from the head man to begin serving. Any infraction of this rule would mean only one warning. Even the First Lady keeps her eye on the head man near the end of the dinner for his signal to let her know that all her guests have finished. With this signal she acquaints the President that he may lead the way for coffee.

Grandi had a suave, hand-kissing style, and the ladies appeared very excited. It was amusing to watch some of them flutter as he would kiss their hands. Of course he was slim, dark, and I suppose handsome, and the Old World heel-clicking style did give him a romantic flair. On departing from a room, in the presence of ladies, he would back away about five paces, click his heels, and bow. And before he passed through the doorway he would again click his heels and bow.

The gathering of a state dinner is very colorful. Military aides from all the services in their dress uniforms escort the ladies to the East Room. The husbands always look sort of unattended, tagging along while the ladies swing on the arm of an aide. In the East Room the aide in charge announces their names and another introduces them to their dinner partners. After all the guests have arrived the aides line up on both sides of the red carpet leading from the elevator to the door of the State Dining Room. The dining room doors are opened, the uniformed butlers at their stations, and the head man in the center of the en trance.

Then the President and the First Lady, with their aides, proceed to the East Room through the cordon of aides. The Marine Band in the lobby strikes up *Hail to the Chief* until they arrive at the East Room and the aide in charge announces the President and the First Lady.

Guests file around and when all of them have been received the entire procession returns down the red carpet to the dining room. Guests are given cards showing the position of their seats. After they are all seated the head man signals to start serving the meal.

Chapter 5

FIRST GLIMPSE OF
FRANKLIN DELANO ROOSEVELT

*M*any state dinners were to follow, plus receptions, teas, christenings, birthday parties and farewell dinners. I shall always remember a governors' convention held in Virginia, I believe in the spring of 1932. President Hoover had invited the governors to dine at the White House.

The man being mentioned as likely to be the Democratic candidate for President was the Governor of New York, Franklin D. Roosevelt. We were instructed to have a different type of chair for him and a strong man to attend his chair. The head man said to me, "Fields, I am assigning you to Mr. Roosevelt's chair. They say he is going to be the Democratic candidate for the White House, so he may be the boss around here this time next year."

When the Governor of New York arrived he created a sensation. He came by the south grounds because he would have to use the elevator. Ike Hoover, the chief usher, took his two top doormen, John Mays and Charles Green—one to help the Governor out of his car and the other to man the elevator.

Ike Hoover greeted the Governor and the Governor greeted him like a long-lost friend, shaking hands. Then he turned to Mays and held out his hand, saying, "Well, John Mays, how are you?" You would have thought Mays was an old friend, too, and as they approached the elevator Governor Roosevelt kept up a running conversation.

On reaching the elevator and seeing Green, the Governor gave the same greeting, laughing and talking all the way up. The men were flabbergasted because it had been nearly twenty years since any of them had seen Franklin Roosevelt and they were not prepared for such informality. Soon the White House buzzed with the news. President Hoover seldom spoke to anyone and of course orders were not to speak unless spoken to. When he did speak, it was news.

Next morning at the medicine-ball breakfast everyone chattered about the possibility of the Governor from New York being a presidential candidate. Some thought the Democrats would not dare to nominate an invalid. Others thought he would be easy to defeat since the American people wouldn't elect a disabled man. Others said he had a marvelous torso and a fascinating, warm, sincere voice and smile and he might impress the radio and newsreel audiences. The breakfast ended with the thought that Franklin Roosevelt, despite his infirmities, was no doubt the most exciting among the possible candidates the Democrats might offer up for the slaughter in the 1932 election.

The time came when there was another medicine-ball breakfast. It was the morning after the all-night balloting at the Chicago convention. Breakfast was as usual under the magnolia tree. In the doctor's office there was a radio which had been placed in the window so that it could be heard during the breakfast. The Democrats had nominated the Governor of New York, Franklin D. Roosevelt, as their candidate for President and, with some members of his family, he startled the country by flying to the convention to accept the nomination.

The renomination of President Hoover was merely a formality. *The Literary Digest* had the President away out in front in its prediction polls, but somehow the medicine-ball breakfast group showed signs of anxiety and an effort was made to get Mr. Coolidge to come out in defense of the party's economic program. The former President took his time before he committed himself to making a nationwide broadcast. Well, the former President made his speech and at the medicine-ball breakfast the next morning the table wasn't too enthused over his efforts. But, on the whole, they thought he had helped the cause.

It was rumored around the White House that ex-President Coolidge wasn't too fond of President Hoover. There were many stories about President Coolidge, how he was always nosing around the kitchen and the help's dining room. There is one such story of how, after one of these visits, he told Mrs. Coolidge, "Mamma, those white folks are eating up my maple syrup and the colored folks haven't any on their table."

The White House had two dining rooms for the help. From then on, for fear that the President might pay an unexpected visit, it was seen to that the colored help's table had the same food as appeared on the other dining-room table.

Separate dining rooms for the white and colored help existed until the Roosevelt Administration ended this by the simple process of eliminating white help in household capacities except for the housekeeper. The gardeners, carpenters and electricians did not have their meals in the White House. However, at Hyde Park, whenever the colored help went there to serve the President, they were not permitted to eat in the dining room for the help. They had to eat in the kitchen. Of course at the White House, with Virginia so nearby, the separate dining rooms could be attributed to the influence of that State's policy, but in New York you did not expect this. So I had my reservations concerning the White House as an example for the rest of the country.

The defeat of President Hoover was a shock to most of the people on the staff and of course *The Literary*

Digest lost face for its poll-taking predictions. Somehow I was not too disturbed over the change of Administrations. I still had hopes of being able to return to Boston and to my singing. How, I didn't know, without a job. But I felt that as long as I had a job at the White House, I would not find time to sing or study. So the White House up to this time had not made much of an impression on me except for the Christmas following the election when I was invited to sing in the East Room for the party given for the help. Of course the President and First Lady were absent, but despite this I had my day, and a very appreciative audience gave me reason to believe they enjoyed my renditions. To this day, that afternoon before Christmas Eve in 1932 was the most thrilling experience in all the twenty-one years in the White House.

It was my day off when Mrs. Roosevelt and a newspaper friend of hers, Miss Lorena Hickok, visited the White House, as it is the custom for the incoming First Lady to meet the First Lady and be escorted over the house, to meet the help, and decide about changes, if any. Of course the changes are later communicated to the chief usher.

When this list arrived it included the white chambermaids, chief cook, second cook and kitchen maids, all Irish girls who had come to the White House during the Coolidge Administration. Mrs. Roosevelt brought a housekeeper and her husband, Mr. and Mrs. Nesbitt. Mr. Nesbitt took over the storeroom where many of the personal presents for the first family and other materials were received. Mrs. Roosevelt also brought Miss Ida Allen as head cook; Mrs. Elizabeth Moore, second cook; McDuffie, a valet, and his wife, Mrs. Lizzie McDuffie, as a maid; and two butlers, James Mingo and James Reynolds. Ellis Sampson, the head butler, had been transferred and we all assumed that one of the men Mrs. Roosevelt was bringing would be the head butler.

On the morning of the inauguration Ellis served breakfast and told the President and Mrs. Hoover goodby. He had a job in the Treasury Department. No one, including Encarnación, the second man, knew exactly what to expect. He had no instructions to take over, yet we all expected him to take charge, at least for Inauguration Day.

Chapter 6

F.D.R. BECOMES PRESIDENT—AND I BE-COME CHIEF BUTLER

*M*arch 4, 1933, my first inauguration, was not only a hard, long day but one filled with mixed emotions and confusion. No one had a plan of what to do except that we did have a menu from Mrs. Roosevelt. For luncheon she had ordered 50 covers, and bouillon, salmon salad, chicken salad, whole-wheat and white-bread-and-butter sandwiches, coffee and tea and plenty of milk. She added ice cream and cake.

There were to be 3,000 covers for tea with assorted sandwiches, buttered nut bread, tea, coffee, punch, cake and cookies. The dinner menu was oyster stew, crackers, scrambled eggs and sausages, fried potatoes, creamed chicken, peas, buttered rolls, buttered biscuits, jellies and jams, charlotte russe and coffee.

For luncheon she didn't want any tables set up, but just to have a few tables nearby. We had a buffet in the center of the dining room. It was a sick-looking table with the chicken salad, salmon salad, bread-and-butter sandwiches, coffee, tea and plenty of milk.

The President came into the dining room on Mr. James Roosevelt's arm. We hustled a table to a spot he requested. Encarnación served the President his bouillon and I rushed over with Mrs. Roosevelt's, but when I reached her she merely smiled and moved away to the table and started serving tea and coffee to the guests.

I stood there holding her bouillon. Well, we were flabbergasted. A First Lady, with all the help we had, rushing off to serve the guests, and the help didn't know what to do! She was really in our way and the order of service was disrupted. No one gave any priority to the President. The guests took what they wanted and we just tried to do our best and acted as if we knew what it was all about.

Someone asked for ice cream before the bouillon had been finished. In fact, we never knew what was what after the First Lady started serving at the buffet table. The guests finished with their lunch and were leaving without waiting for the President to finish.

Encarnación said, "I don't understand these people. They eat ice cream with their bouillon."

If that luncheon was such confusion, how were we to set up the horseshoe table for 75 people to serve oyster stew, scrambled eggs and sausages, fried potatoes, creamed chicken, buttered rolls and biscuits and buttered peas?

Encarnación asked Ike Hoover, "How do we serve such a dinner at a horseshoe table?"

Mr. Hoover said, "Your guess is just as good as mine."

I spoke up and said, "Connie, this isn't a formal dinner, even though they will all be in evening clothes. This is just a New England countryman's supper, so do not use the gold service. Use the silver. After we serve the oyster stew and crackers, serve the scrambled eggs, sausages, fried potatoes, creamed chicken, peas, hot rolls, biscuits, jellies and jams."

He said, "All on one plate?"

I said, "Yes; and do not expect to serve demitasses. Have coffee and tea and milk ready. After passing the bread and jams, place plates of bread and jams at intervals on the tables."

Before we had finished serving the oyster stew, Mrs. Roosevelt said, "We will have the coffee and tea and milk with the dinner."

So Connie said to me, "Mr. Fields, you were right."

I said, "Yes, Connie, these people are going to throw Old Man Protocol and formality right out the window, from what little I have seen."

Well, the guests finished their dinners just as they willed, saying, "I must be going." Sometimes Mrs. Roosevelt would say, "Franklin, Joe"—or Jane—"is leaving now." The President would smile and say, "Well, Joe, it was good of you to come. We'll see you later. Have a good time."

This was going on all through the dinner—And to think that just twenty-four hours earlier no one would have thought of leaving the table before the President!

I have told you about the luncheon and dinner, but to my mind the worst attempt at serving a party was the tea that afternoon for 3,000. It was chaos. In the center of the State Dining Room was a table about twenty feet long and in the small dining room was another table not quite so long. In no time the tables were completely surrounded by guests, eight and ten deep. No one could get to the table and those who were there couldn't get out, nor could they drink their tea or coffee because the crowd was pinning them fast. The butlers couldn't get to the tables to replenish or remove the soiled dishes, and many guests left in disgust. But to those in charge it was the best that could be done with a bad situation. Little did I realize that four years later on an inaugural day I would be given the chance to prove whether or not I could plan a better system of handling large parties at the White House.

Inauguration Day of 1933 was on Saturday, and from 6:30 A.M. until 1 A.M. Sunday had been our workday. Every room in the White House was filled and

Mrs. Roosevelt had scheduled breakfast for eight o'clock the next morning. There were to be trays for the President and Mrs. Sara Roosevelt, the President's mother.

Right off we learned that being on time for meals was not one of the Roosevelts' virtues, and in all the twelve years, I can count on one hand the times that they were on time for a meal. Ida Allen, Mrs. Roosevelt's cook, took over for the breakfast and she seemed not to be in the least disturbed. She smiled when she was told that breakfast would be at eight o'clock. It was eight o'clock before she started the sausages.

Poor Encarnación was upset. He said, "We sure do not want to be late on their first morning."

She said, "Don't worry. You will be serving breakfast at twelve if I know these people." And she knew them, for we served our last breakfast at noon Sunday.

I had often thought what a relief it would be not to have to serve the medicine-ball breakfast. But after just one or two mornings of serving a Roosevelt breakfast I would sit back and say, "Oh, for the good old days!" However, one is lost if one isn't quick to adjust, and before I knew it I had become a part of what at first struck you as impossible.

These Roosevelts were a fascinating family—they did not seem to give a hoot if you did or did not like them, for they were enjoying themselves. The Roosevelts were not hard to please. I did not have to worry about noises in the pantry as in the Hoover Administration when I had to tiptoe while washing the dishes. In fact, we were told not to wash dishes during the serving of dinner. (The pantry crew would ease a few through, for, with dinner served at eight o'clock and seven courses, there would be quite a pile of dishes to clean up.) Well, the Roosevelts kept up so much noise in the dining room that washing dishes in the pantry did not create a problem.

The butlers did not have to stand in the dining room during a family meal or an informal guest dinner. Mrs. Roosevelt had a bell, but many a time we could hardly hear it in the pantry. We would peek through the glass in the dining room and keep our eyes on Mrs. Roosevelt to watch when she would ring. So within a few days this family had the old White House rocking with their gaiety and laughter.

On March 18 Ike Hoover called the staff of butlers together and said, "Encarnación, you have been acting as chief butler for these few days, as you are the assistant chief. You are still the assistant chief butler. Fields, you are the chief butler."

So on that day I took full charge of the White House staff of butlers. I had not expressed any desire for the job and was most surprised. I could not very well say No, for the extra money would help out the family, but, with the new job, I knew I would have no time for singing.

Encarnación was a most excellent assistant, but he was no longer a young man. He had served the Coolidges and Hoovers and, though these Administrations were busy, there was a quiet routine about the entertaining. He was bewildered by this new lack of routine when we had to anticipate last-minute changes. Nothing upsets help more than to disturb a table setting five or ten minutes before the time for the meal. I was likely to have to add five or six to the setting, or remove that number. Often the President and guests would be coming into the dining room before we could complete the changes.

The Roosevelts used the small dining room, better known as the breakfast room, for all meals except breakfast and formal dinners of over thirty people. Of course all state affairs were held in the State Dining Room. Breakfast was served in the West Hall and each morning we moved furniture to set up for a number that could only be estimated from a note the ushers would post on a bulletin board, written by Mrs. Roosevelt. That is, if we could read her writing. Any way I would take it, I was playing a guessing game as to how many to expect and what she meant for me to do.

The breakfast coffee cups were the oversized hunting breakfast cups and the traditional Roosevelt coffee was half coffee and half hot milk. Of course there was cream for those who took cream. Mrs. Roosevelt always poured the coffee and sometimes there would be so many of these huge cups that we had to place a side table near her, for we could not pile them on the table beside her. She used left- and right-hand pots to execute the pouring of coffee and milk.

The President always had a tray in his room which McDuffie, the valet, would take up. The coffee for the President was a deep black French roast, prepared in the kitchen. We roasted the green coffee beans to any degree we wanted. The President's coffee, however, was a much deeper roast than we used for the family, and it was freshly ground. A coffeemaker was placed on the tray so the President could control the brewing of his coffee.

Since breakfast was more or less a state of confusion, this was just the beginning. Each day was just the same. In comparison with the Hoover Administration, it was like being used to dining in the Waldorf-Astoria, and then in a cafeteria. Though the food was good and wholesome, let us say its presentation was poorly done, with no desire to please or excite the appetite.

Chapter 7

PRESIDENT ROOSEVELT'S GUESTS

aS IF the Roosevelt family were not large enough, from time to time we had others who required special care and attention, and often they were more difficult to please than the family. The first of these permanent guests was Mr. Louis Howe, the President's chief adviser of political know-how. He was catered to by all the members of the family, admired, and to all appearances loved and respected for his advice.

Mr. Howe was not a well man and most of the time he kept to his room, which was the small Lincoln Room. He had the most unusual breakfast. I did not wonder at his not being too well. He would have cold codfish cakes with catchup and Tabasco sauce, and cornmeal pone made with white meal with no shortening and so tight it could hardly be broken with both hands. And he smoked as he ate.

This gentleman from Indiana had a gruff way about him and he was just as gruff with the President as with anyone else. One day during the serving of tea to the President and the British ambassador he neared the room and heard voices. He inquired, "Who is in there with Franklin?"

I said it was the British ambassador.

He said, "I want to see Franklin. Tell him when he is through with that bloke to come to my room."

So I thought, "Me tell the President that you want him to come to your room?" I was flabbergasted, but when the ambassador left I told the President that Mr. Howe wanted to see him.

He said, "Louis wants to see me? Where is he?"

I said, "In his room, sir."

The President said, "Get McDuffie." I called McDuffie and the President said, "Bring the chair, Mac. I got to go to Louis' room. He wants to see me."

So that was Louis Howe. When he sent for any member of the family, there was no hesitation. They went and they listened. Mr. Howe was really a member of the Roosevelt family rather than an outsider. He was the adviser of the family, and everyone would go to him to talk over any affair—especially those concerning public relations. Mr. Howe would tell in a very gruff way whether a thing was right or wrong and everyone seemed to take it with a smile. They would say, "All right, Louis—if you say so, Louis—it must be all right." Mr. Howe also had a big influence over the entire staff, and everyone would say of a problem, "See what Louis has to say about it."

Another permanent guest was Miss Le Hand, the President's personal secretary. She had quarters which had been the housekeeper's in the Hoover Administration. Miss Le Hand was a very pleasant and lady-like person and was very easy to please. She remained, like Mr. Howe, until she lost her health, and she was loved by all of the servants.

One of Mrs. Roosevelt's first acts of social change was to lift the ban on ladies smoking. Though Mrs. Roosevelt did not really smoke, she would ask for the cigarettes to be passed and would take one and go through the motions of smoking. Anyone knew she did not really know how to smoke. After she had established the custom of ladies smoking in the White House she stopped taking the smokes when they were passed.

The first formal dinner was the Cabinet dinner. This proved to be quite a task for me to maneuver diplomatically for the type of dinner that would be expected in the White House. Mrs. Nesbitt, the housekeeper, Miss Allen, the cook, and myself would meet in the housekeeper's office and plan the meals. The housekeeper's idea of a state dinner was that of an inn's banquet, and the cook was going along with the idea. Food was to be served on plates individually. I was told there would be no waste, as in the Hoover Administration, and that Mrs. Roosevelt did not believe in elaborate dinners.

I told them that the dinner they were planning would certainly greatly change what had usually been expected of the White House and that I was sure Mrs. Roosevelt had dined at the White House and knew the customs. Why not consult her before we submitted menus for her to select?

Mrs. Roosevelt did turn thumbs down on the banquet type of service where food was served in the kitchen on the plates, but she cut off two courses. If there was an entree, soup would usually be cut out. If there were an entree and soup, the fish course would be omitted. And no fruit course.

Soon the word got around that the White House food was terrible and of course the blame was put on Mrs. Nesbitt. The President said he could always tell by the day of the week what he would have for lunch. The Roosevelts could have been the easiest people in the world to plan meals for. They would try almost anything they had not eaten before, and they liked almost everything. So you could plan weeks ahead without repeating and always have a meal that would be exciting and appealing for them.

Mrs. Roosevelt was a moderate eater without any particular fondness for any one kind of food. The President also was a moderate eater, but he had a particular fondness for all wild game, curried chicken, and pigs' feet in a sweet-sour sauce. It was this type of pigs' feet that he requested to be served at luncheon for just the Prime Minister, Winston Churchill, and himself.

Princess Martha of Norway, who lived at Pookshill, Maryland, during the war, had a cook who often prepared pigs' feet in this style and she had brought the President this dish. He had a twinkle in his eye when he said, "Let's have them for luncheon tomorrow for the Prime Minister."

When luncheon was served and the Prime Minister started to help himself, he inquired, "What is this?"

He was told, "Sir, this is pigs' feet."

He said, "Pigs' feet? I never heard of them," and then heartily helped himself. After tasting them he said, "Very good, but sort of slimy."

The President laughed and said, "Yes, they are a bit, but I am fond of them. Sometime we will have some of them fried."

Whereupon the Prime Minister replied, "No, thank you. I do not believe I would care for them fried." Then they both had a hearty laugh.

Prohibition had been abolished, making it necessary to send for barrels of glassware which had been packed up and stored away when the prohibition amendment went into effect. We found some rare cut glass and crystal dating back to the Harrison Administration, including wine-glasses of all descriptions. In no time at all gifts from wine manufacturers poured into the White

House—even Japanese saki. Very little of it was palatable for the table, but we would serve a spiked punch and a fruit punch at receptions, so I experimented with combinations of wine to develop a punch to use up the gift wines.

The spiked punch always went over big. Even with the most sedate groups, when we served 35 to 45 gallons of fruit punch we would need an average of 110 gallons of spiked punch for a crowd of 1,200, and most likely I would have to draw on a reserve supply. I first thought that, because of the newness of lifting the prohibition law, this consumption of spiked punch would wear off, but in the years to follow the averages kept steady.

Chapter 8

OFFICIAL RECEPTIONS

There were five official receptions each social season—the Diplomatic, Judicial, Congressional, Departmental, and the Army and Navy. You could grade these receptions on estimates of quantities and qualities of food and drinks. The diplomats never eat much or drink too much because these people are continually on the go and, come tomorrow, they must do this same thing over. At the Judicial receptions the higher echelon, like the diplomats, eat little and drink lightly, but the lower echelon can sort of step it up for you. So the general pattern of Judicial, Congressional and Departmental receptions is that business will be slow around the punch bowls until after the bigwigs have been down the line. However, the Army and Navy must have had very few bigwigs or big brass, for within fifteen minutes after the line started moving the rush would be on until the end. For the newspaper and radio press parties and receptions you opened the doors and tried to keep the bowls filled.

So I made my estimates by what information the social room would supply. If it was a political club, church organization or delegates at a convention, I had to remember that any affair at the White House is really an outing plus the fact of taking home to little Ann or Mary a cooky from the White House. Eighty percent will take two helpings, 75 percent three helpings, and another 30 percent four helpings. I have seen people load their plates with five and six sandwiches and cakes. The more varieties of cakes, cookies and sandwiches there are, the more some people just must sample each kind.

Mrs. Roosevelt invented the double-header teas. I am sure most First Ladies called it a day after receiving 400 or 500 people in an afternoon. However, Mrs. Roosevelt would schedule two different groups—one at 4:00 P.M. and another at 5:00 P.M. There would be 400 or 500 in each group.

This meant that after the first group was cleaned out, you had about thirty minutes to re-dress your table with fresh china, cloths and food. I was told by old-timers that it could not be done. I had the carpenters build a 40-foot table across the west wall in front of the fireplace in the State Dining Room. The table was filled with assortments of cookies, cakes, sandwiches, nuts and candy. All the serving tables at the sides and end of the dining room would also be filled with this assortment.

I had six services of trays, holding ten cups of tea or coffee. These were passed to the guests as they entered the dining room, with a crew of girls pouring tea and coffee in the small dining room which was used as a serving pantry. Each trip to the state room by the waiters meant 60 cups of tea and coffee and six trips could be made in twelve minutes and 360 guests served. This left only 70 cups of tea or coffee to be served at either end of the table, yet the guests were all served and had time to eat. As soon as they finished the aides and ushers moved them along, explaining there was another party waiting.

When the chief usher told me Mrs. Roosevelt's plans for these double-header teas he said she wanted the cost to be kept at the minimum. All sandwiches had to be prepared in the pantry. No buying from a caterer. Sandwiches that cost from $5 to $10 a hundred I found could be made by a pantry crew for $1.50 a hundred, including labor.

When I first went to M. I. T., I was told by Mr. Parris, "If you can prepare for six, you can prepare for six thousand. You merely multiply." During those days most anyone was being invited to the White House, and without a doubt this is the way it should be, for, after all, the White House belongs to the people. I am sure Mrs. Roosevelt didn't refuse any group admittance, and nothing delighted her more than to give them a sip of tea, coffee or lemonade and cookies. But even just to hand 500 to 800 people a glass of water means work.

Mrs. Roosevelt had great stamina and a capacity for greeting people, and a big party today didn't mean that she would rest tomorrow. When I finished today's party, I merely crossed it off my list, for tomorrow there might be a formal luncheon for 50 or 60 ladies, a social family dinner at night with perhaps 25 to 30 guests, and a movie starting near ten o'clock with refreshments afterward. And again the next day another double-header tea, if she didn't take off on a trip somewhere and want a 6:30 breakfast. She seemed never to tire.

When I had finished a party, before leaving for home, I would check my orders for the next day, check the list of help required and assignments and make up the list for the Secret Service and police guards. One seldom hears a compliment, but just let something go wrong, and one will hear the bad news. So I checked and double-checked. Even if the President and the First Lady were pleased (and they were always the easiest to please), it was a day of real accomplishment when the help, too, were pleased with my efforts.

The mass production of teas and receptions created a souvenir seekers' problem. Mostly it was linen tea napkins and the less expensive electroplated silver used for such large parties. We were not in the least bit snobbish, but we had to face the facts of life.

It was really commendable of the First Lady to invite so many people of different walks of life to a tea or reception. Many of the Washington elite made snob-bish remarks that everyone was going to the White House. One lady said that she had let her maid off for the afternoon, since she was invited to a tea at the White House. To her amazement, she saw the maid in the receiving line ahead of her. This was more than she could stand, so she feigned a sudden illness and left.

There is no truth in that story, I am sure, but people will talk.

Souvenir seekers posed a diplomatic problem. I dared not accuse anyone of taking a souvenir. Like the time when a lady guest had packed a silver tray in a bag to take with her. She was having trouble closing the bag and in the meantime breakfast was announced, so she asked the maid if she would fasten the bag.

The maid started to rearrange the clothing so that the bag would close and discovered a fourteen-inch silver tray bought for the White House in 1898 and inscribed "The President's House." She called me and asked what she must do.

She said, "Maybe Mrs. Roosevelt gave the tray to her. Should I tell the chief usher?"

I told her to say nothing to anyone and that I would take the tray back to the pantry. I was sure Mrs. Roosevelt had not given the lady the tray, for not even Mrs. Roosevelt could dispose of it. The White House and all its furnishings were merely being loaned to her by the people of the United States while the President was working for them.

The maid said, "What if she should look into her bag before she leaves and ask about it?"

I laughed and said, "The lady will never question you about this, and if she ever returns as a guest she will be ashamed to look you in your eyes."

The Roosevelts inaugurated so many social events, like the movie stars' luncheon and the luncheon the Cabinet ladies gave for the Senate ladies. I should like to tell about the Cabinet ladies' luncheon for the Senate ladies. This was always a garden-party luncheon, weather permitting.

First we would have a luncheon for the Cabinet ladies at which they planned the menu for the party for the Senate ladies and decided which part of the menu each Cabinet lady would donate. Here I must say these Cabinet ladies were no different from any group of church ladies getting ready for a church supper. Some ladies could always be depended on to supply quantity and quality, while with others no one could know just how much they would bring. I will not have to consult my diary to recall the ladies of the Cabinet who brought quantities and quality food nor to recall the ladies who more or less were a little sparing.

Those like Mrs. Morgenthau, Mrs. Woodring, Mrs. Hull, Mrs. Garner, Mrs. Ickes and Mrs. Swanson always made up for the ladies who happened to be a wee bit sparing. The most sparing of the lot seemed to be Miss Perkins, the Secretary of Labor. Usually she would supply a spongecake, made by a local chain store with the brand name on it. After all, she was a Cabinet member and a very busy lady.

After two or three years Mrs. Roosevelt suggested that she supply whatever menu the Cabinet ladies decided on, the cost to be shared equally. This worked out much better and it was easier for us.

The movie stars' luncheons started with the President's birthday ball for the March of Dimes. These luncheons always afforded the help a bit of excitement. They were more excited over them than over the visit of a king or queen. We all had our favorites among the stars and all of them at some time or other were lunch eon guests. Melvyn Douglas and his wife, who was a congresswoman from California, were often house guests. James Cagney, Errol Flynn, Robert Taylor, Ralph Bellamy, George Raft, Irene Dunne, Paulette Goddard and Edward G. Robinson—to tell the truth, there were too many to mention. The ones that impressed me most were Wallace Beery, who kept complaining that his feet hurt, and Marie Dressler, who remarked that she thought me handsome and that I should be in Hollywood. I was flattered and she will always live in my memory.

Edward G. Robinson, when he was a guest for an inaugural affair, came behind the scenes and met the help in the pantry.

Mrs. Roosevelt and members of the family would attend the March-of-Dimes balls at the different hotels after a birthday dinner for the President at the White House. This dinner usually brought most of the Roosevelt clan together, plus old Hyde Park and Albany friends—a group which always included the Morgenthaus. Presents would be piled on the table, on the floor, and under the table at the President's chair.

Many politicians often spoke of the President as being a money spender. Perhaps so with other people's money, but a party of this type came out of the family budget and when I would inquire of the President if he wanted champagne he would say, "How many do we expect?"

He could estimate to a drink how many bottles to use and he would add, "Do not pour too often and be sure to have enough left to fill the glasses for the toasts."

He had the frugality of a Vermont Yankee. He usually made his own cocktails and never made any more than enough to go around. If he made seconds, he would get the count needed. You never found even the essence of a drink left in a cocktail shaker.

The President was a very able carver of all kinds of wild game. He delighted in carving for all family parties and no man could get more off a pheasant, duck or turkey. He would scrape the carcass of a bird white before he would ask for another. Many times we would have birds for the boys of the family to carve as well as the President when the parties were so large, because, the way the President shaved a bird, dinner would be slow in coming if only one person carved.

The family always got a kick out of comparing the number of guests the President could serve from one turkey with the number any of the boys could serve. As I have said before, the Roosevelts were a fun-loving family and they always enjoyed themselves immensely at their family parties. No guest could stand back and not take part.

Chapter 9

INTERNATIONAL PARADE

*J*UNE of 1939 started the big parade of international entertaining. I like to think of the important men and women for whose comfort and services I was responsible during their visits at the White House. The premier attraction in 1939 was the visit of the King and Queen of England.

Washington went all out in its reception for the King and Queen of England in the spring of 1939, with the red carpet and all the trimmings. At the White House we were well informed through the State Department and the British embassy about the likes and dislikes of Their Majesties.

But we had our problems. The White House is actually not large enough to accommodate such a large entourage. Besides the king and queen there were the lady in waiting, the aides, the royal servants and servants to the royal servants—like the royal boot black and his aide, the queen's royal maid and her aides.

One bit of information really flubbed the dub. We were told to have bed warmers for the king's and queen's beds. Can you imagine using a bed warmer in June in Washington? We deliberated for a long time as to whether they were confused and meant a bed cooler, because there certainly would be no need for a warmer in June in Washington. In England, however, I understand that nights can be cool in June.

The usual procedure is for important state guests to arrive at the White House at teatime, following the reception through downtown streets and public demonstration of welcome. After a formal tea the President and First Lady entertain at a state dinner, then the guests spend the night, departing next day for Blair House across the street for the rest of their visit.

But the King and Queen of England stayed at the White House until their departure for New York and Hyde Park with the President and Mrs. Roosevelt. The king was a retiring, frail-looking man. The queen, with her pleasant expression, was mild-mannered in appearance. They were likeable people, without affectation, and I admired their royal dignity.

President Roosevelt was very much interested in this visit and took over planning the menu for the state dinner. He actually went over the menu personally. In all the twelve years of his Administration I dare say this was the only dinner that compared in dignity and quality with the White House dinners of the Hoover Administration.

The President wanted terrapin à la Maryland for the first course, but we did not have any terrapin dishes. When the President heard this he asked about it and I took the opportunity to tell him of the inadequate equipment of the kitchen for entertaining the rulers of the world with the dignity becoming to the wealthiest country in the world. The gold flatware lacked soup-spoons, fish forks and knives. We had to use salad forks for dessert forks, and this meant washing the forks and spoons between courses before we could serve the fish or the dessert.

He said, "How horrible. But you know, if we were to ask for all those things you say we need, the politicians would make headlines out of the gold tableware being bought for the White House."

I said I realized this, but the newspapers had been sort of belittling our furnishings in comparison with the British embassy and the elegance and royal traditions of our visitors.

The President smiled and said, "I know how you feel, but at least I am sure we can arrange to get the terrapin dishes."

The dinner was a success. Besides an elegant course of terrapin I was, for once, able to buy enough Belgian hothouse grapes not only to decorate the table but also to make a service of fruit bowls to pass as a fruit course.

I don't remember any other time since the Hoover Administration when this had happened or ever did happen again. We had been taking Tokay grapes and wiring them together to form clusters to decorate the tall fruit dishes on the table.

At the center of the horseshoe table there was usually one high-backed chair on each side for the President and First Lady, but the ruler of a country rates a high-backed chair. So there were two chairs with high backs on each side of the table that night. The President and the queen sat on one side and the king and First Lady on the other side.

On this occasion we changed the form of service. The President and king were served at the same time, and the First Lady and queen were served at the same time. The dinner began at eight o'clock with the aides in their colorful uniforms, ladies in beautiful gowns especially bought for the occasion, and with royalty present everything seemed just a little bit more exciting.

The queen had a pillow she used in the car seat, and shortly after she was seated she requested this pillow. I think it prevented her from sitting too low in the car or at the table. So the President asked me to have her pillow brought. I sent one of the men to her maid for it, and as the Queen of England lifted herself I gently slipped the pillow on the chair.

We had a schedule to keep. My orders were to have the dining room cleared by ten o'clock, for 300 more guests were coming for the musicale after the dinner.

When the President tapped his goblet of heavy cut glass that rang like a beautiful bell the table hushed to quietness. Then the President offered a toast to Their Majesties, the king and queen, and to the people of England.

In response the king stood and offered a toast to the President and First Lady and to the people of the United States. If there had been complete quietness when the President offered his toast, it was even more noticeable when the king spoke. The king had had the affliction of stammering and I never felt so deeply moved in my life as, standing behind the President's chair, I watched this man of royal birth uttering his words with deliberation and dignity. His face showed a determined effort as he paused after each word, but without any hesitation or stammering.

To face an audience with this impediment of speech must have required great courage, willpower and long hours of training. Perhaps it was my imagination, but the guests all appeared too alert in listening for the impediment of speech—or else I was judging others by myself.

After the toasts Mrs. Roosevelt and the queen led the ladies to the Green Parlor for coffee, and the President and the king led the gentlemen for coffee and liqueurs. For the concert we had Kate Smith, Lawrence Tibbett and Marian Anderson. Needless to say, the concert was a success and the artists were presented to the king and queen. After the musicale we served champagne punch to more than 300 guests.

At 1:00 A.M., before closing shop, I went over my instructions for the next morning's breakfasts. I had these instructions:

"Her Majesty, the queen—8:00 A.M. a small tray of tea; 9:00 A.M. tray of tea and fresh fruit, nothing else; 10:00 A.M., have a small decanter of sherry in Their Majesties' sitting room. Also be prepared with a tray of tea in case Their Majesties ask for it."

This message was from the lady in waiting. There were no orders for the king's breakfast. One thing was certain: breakfast was to be a little vague. But, including the lady in waiting, His Majesty's aide and royal servants, we served tea, more tea and still nothing but tea for breakfast, which was a novelty for us.

We had luncheon for the royal party and the presidential family, and a tea in the south grounds that afternoon so that some of the Cabinet members and heads of Government departments could be presented to Their Majesties. Each department head was seated with the royal party for a short time while the king would ask questions about the working of their departments—especially the WPA and Social Security, for they were new adventures in government. On the third evening the king and queen departed for New York and from there to Hyde Park.

It was indeed an honor and a pleasure to have had this opportunity to play my small part in this important event. The king and queen were two grand people, but their royal servants could have stayed in England. They required more service than the king and queen, the lady in waiting or His Majesty's aides. The royal maid to the queen had two assistants, and she was a real browbeater. She would storm at the girls and they darted around like scared rabbits. In short, that royal maid to a royal lady was an overbearing snob. She criticized about everything we did with a sharp tongue. She was our guest and we no doubt would not ever see her again, but once was enough.

Chapter 10

THE SHADOW OF WAR

J HE Hitler shadow was looming over Europe. Little did I realize that within a few months this royal couple, their nation and all Europe would be in a death struggle to survive. By September Hitler struck Poland, and England declared war on Germany.

Shortly after Dunkirk Ambassador Kennedy returned for a conference with the President, and after the conference Harry Hopkins asked, "How did you make out with Kennedy?"

The President replied, "Oh, I can handle Joe, but you know it is a shame that a man as smart as Kennedy is so blinded by his Irish hatred of England that he thinks England will be finished within the next two months. And he would not mind a bit. I did leave him with this thought: that when the liberties of forty million people on the British Isles are threatened, we are more than interested."

The President's name was offered at the Democratic National Convention for the third term and he was drafted over Garner and Farley. Mr. Willkie captured the Republican top spot and the race was on.

The President seemed to be very much impressed by Mr. Willkie, and after the election invited him to an off-the-record dinner in the Oval Room on the second floor. The President had been tipped off that Willkie was very fond of terrapin, and as we had no terrapin we rushed off to Harvey's, then one of Washington's finest eating places which catered to the diplomats with rare dishes. Mr. Willkie entered by the back door and went up the elevator to the second floor, where Mr. Hopkins ushered him in to the President.

Cocktails mixed by the President were served and just the three gentlemen had dinner. Mr. Hopkins began the conversation by saying, "I wanted you and the President to get together, for I think you are as important as the President in your approach to the new ideology of government which, as you know, isn't the Old Guard Republican viewpoint. As you know, also, the President doesn't have the viewpoint of the conservative Democrats."

These remarks brought from Mr. Willkie a sudden explosive, "Oh! I'll be damned!" He pushed his chair back from the table and said, "What do you guys have up your sleeves? Let's lay the cards on the table."

I heard no more of this conversation, for it was necessary for me to leave the room. I certainly would have liked to hear more, for this man from Indiana seemed to be very explosive. Mr. Willkie was never mentioned again after this conference in my presence, nor did I ever know the full reason for his off-the record dinner appointment.

We were serving a luncheon party for Mrs. Roosevelt and the President was having lunch in the study on the second floor on Sunday, December 7, 1941, when the news really started things buzzing around the old house. The President called in the Cabinet and leaders of Congress. The Japanese envoy was called in and I understood from the usher, Mr. Claunch, that the President read the blast act to Mr. Saburo Kurusu, the envoy from Japan.

The President remained in his study. I heard him remark as further details continued to come in about the destruction of the fleet, "My God! How did it happen? I will go down in disgrace."

When I left the White House for home near one o'clock the next morning people were crowding the street in Lafayette Square, watching the White House. I do not know what they expected to see at that hour of the morning. The next day the President went before Congress stating that a state of war existed with the imperial government of Japan.

If I had thought the days of the early New Deal were busy, from then on I really had something to learn. For instance, on December 22 I thought that my daily detail was completed at 6:00 P.M. and was preparing to leave for home when my phone rang. I was told that an important guest was expected at about 7:oo P.M. The number in his party would be anywhere from 25 to 40 people, and the name of the guest was off the record.

Well, when the guest arrived one look told us that he was the Prime Minister of England, Winston Churchill.

This man Churchill was a dynamic personality. I felt it when he stepped into the room. His manner was typical of John Bull himself, with a jovial, ironic wit, a gruff, outspoken personality that could wax warm at times, yet I was sure that underneath it was cold, factual and determined. His entourage occupied the entire east wing of the White House.

His was a healthy appetite. On his breakfast tray I was instructed to have something hot, something cold, two kinds of fresh fruit, a tumbler of orange juice and a pot of frightfully weak tea. For "something hot" he had eggs, bacon or ham, and toast. For "something cold" he had two kinds of cold meats with English mustard and two kinds of fruit plus a tumbler of sherry. This was breakfast. At lunch he had Scotch and soda. For dinner always champagne, and after dinner, brandy. Then during the evening more Scotch and soda.

The Prime Minister would wear an air-raid suit around the house, attending most of the morning conference in this outfit. He would have conferences with his staff in which Lord Mountbatten was an important figure and the President would have conferences with his staff, including Admiral Leahy, Admiral King and General Marshall. Later the two combined staffs would go into conference together which could last and last.

During this stay many people who knew that the Prime Minister was a house guest were disappointed, on being invited to the White House, not to meet the President and the Prime Minister. Except for official occasions, they did not eat in the dining room. By dining together with a few of their advisers much time was saved. Mr. Churchill was to be with us for quite a few days.

At one time during this visit he left and went to the British embassy to avoid meeting Mme. Chiang Kai-shek. I heard Mrs. Roosevelt in the West Hall telling him that she wished he would stay. Mr. Churchill replied, "No. Thank you very much, but I know I couldn't stand that woman and I might not be able to hold my temper, or rather my tongue."

The next time he left us was when Mr. Crim, the head usher, called me and said, "The President wants you to get a crew together for a secret mission, destination unknown." The crew had to be selected at once. Each person was to leave his job and go home and stay there until a Secret Service man would come for him. The men were to pack for a stay of ten or fifteen days. When the Secret Service man arrived he would tell them what to do. No further information could be given.

Mr. Crim said, "The person to be cared for is a very important man and the President would appreciate it very much if you went in charge of the detail yourself." Of course the President had but to order, but men of great quality have a way of giving others the feeling that they are aiding them and that they are needed.

This was on Saturday, January 3, 1942, at 2:00 P.M. I selected my crew, called them together and gave them the instructions just as I had received them. I was asked, "What can we tell our families?"

I said, "There isn't anything you can tell them except that you are going on a mission for the President. Where, when and for how long, you do not know. But, by all means, remain at home." Those who needed tools I told to get their tools, to answer no questions and to get out of the house as quietly as possible without attracting attention.

I called in my first assistant, Charles Ficklin, and told him I would be gone for a few days and to take over. Then I went home and waited.

Sunday, January 4, at about 2:00 P.M. a Secret Serv ice man whom I had never seen before rang my door bell and presented his I.D. card. I grabbed my bag and said good-by to my wife and daughter. Then we went to the Washington Union Station, where we entered by the official driveway.

The Secret Service instructed my crew to wait in the concourse and took me into the stationmaster's office.

In a small room off this office he gave me my instructions and the tickets. He told me to read the instructions and then destroy them.

After reading the instructions I went back to the crew and took them aboard a train. I was the only one in the party who knew our destination, but I was not to tell the others until we arrived there. My instructions were to get off the train near Fort Lauderdale, Florida. The conductor would let me know when we arrived there, which would be about noon on Monday. There we were to be met by another Secret Service man. The rest of our trip would be made by car.

We reached the place near Fort Lauderdale at 12:25. The man who met us was not a Secret Service man, but identified himself as the caretaker of a home owned by Mrs. Campbell, a relative of Mr. Stettinius, of the State Department. Her house was at Pompano on the sea and he said we were going there. His name was Edwin Lewis.

He was anxious to know whom we were going to take care of. Since Mr. Stettinius had made the arrangements, he was sure it would be the President. I told him I did not know, and at this he smiled. But I truly did not know.

However, I was guessing and when we arrived at Pompano the Secret Service detail told me to be prepared for about 15 or 20 people. Well, my job was cut out for me, for it was nearly 2 P.M. The plane was due to arrive with the important guest at seven o'clock and dinner was scheduled for eight o'clock.

Mr. Crim, the head usher, had said that the Secret Service would arrange credit and that the house was completely ready to occupy. But the Secret Service had not been so instructed. With the help of the caretaker, I made a quick check of linens, china and sup plies and sleeping quarters. Lo and behold, we even had to set up beds, and I had to drive fifteen miles for provisions with no credit credentials. Someone had failed somewhere along the detail.

I did not know just what to do, for I had only $100 of my own to buy whiskey, brandy, champagne and food for from 15 to 20 people. The Secret Service man in charge told me he had no way to get to the stores because all the cars and trucks were needed to meet the plane. He said perhaps the caretaker could help me out. Mr. Lewis said he would take me in his car to the markets and stores. I showed him my White House I.D. card and asked if he would take me to Mrs. Campbell's tradesmen and vouch for me in securing provisions. He did, and we had no trouble. In fact, the tradespeople were most cordial. In many cases they invited me behind their counters to select whatever I wanted.

When the guests arrived I was not in the least surprised to find that it was Mr. Churchill and his party. Besides the Secret Service detail, this included the Scotland Yard chief and his detail, the Prime Minister's naval aide, his secretary, his physician, his valet and other staff members.

Well, I had everything for the dinner except the champagne, for which I made my apologies to the Prime Minister. This little town did not supply champagne for their trade, and by the time it had arrived from Miami it was too late for dinner. The day ended at 2 A.M. when we had bedded the Prime Minister.

Next morning I was in the pantry when I heard a voice roar, "I say—Where is everybody?"

I answered as I entered the dining room off the pantry, "Good morning, Mr. Prime Minister."

There he stood in his bare feet, looking like a pudgy, mischievous boy with a smile. He said, "Good morning. I say, can you expedite my man, Saunders, for me? And have the morning papers arrived?"

He was very complimentary about the dinner we had served the night before. I had had a standing roast of beef with Yorkshire pudding and horse-radish sauce, and of course at any meal—even breakfast—I always served English mustard to the Prime Minister. He mentioned only the roast beef and Yorkshire pudding, saying it helped him to forget the fact that there was no champagne—which to my mind was a reminder to be sure and have champagne for dinner. I assured him there would be champagne that night.

Before we finished out little talk Saunders, the valet, came rushing in. The Prime Minister turned and roared at him, "So you have found your way!"

Saunders was a very nervous little man and he rushed off in a twitter, saying, "Sir, I will have your bath ready in a jiffy." After his bath the Prime Minister would have a tumbler of sherry. Then he was ready for his hearty breakfast.

Shortly after his tray had been returned, my bell rang and the indicator registered the Prime Minister's quarters. I entered the sitting room where he was sitting at the desk. I said, "Did you ring for me, sir?"

He grunted and said, "Yes. I am sure you are aware that I do not like whistling or talking outside my quarters. May I depend on you to take care of this detail?"

I replied, "By all means, Mr. Prime Minister."

Medina, the chef, was great for whistling. He enjoyed whistling Schubert's Serenade, and sometimes he would keep it going for most of the day. In the White House the kitchen was so far from everything that he was never heard except by the crew. Here it was different, so I told Medina, "No more whistling."

But every so often Medina would forget. Most of the times I would stop him. However, one of these times I forgot and, behold, my bell rang. I knew what was up when I saw the indicator. It pointed to the Prime Minister's quarters. Medina was in the midst of his whistling rendition of Schubert's Serenade. On the way to answer the bell I stopped by the kitchen and halted Medina.

Mr. Churchill was in the library reading as I entered. I said, "Yes, Mr. Prime Minister."

For a second or two he looked at me with that Churchill scowl. Maybe he thought this would un nerve me; but after facing men with six- and eight ounce gloves as I had done for a while as a young man in Indiana, knowing their only thought was to beat my brains out for a few dollars and that their reputations were such that they were quite capable of doing it, no mental lashing could unnerve me.

Then he said, "How many stone do you weigh and how tall are you?"

I replied, "Sir, I am not too familiar with the English system of weight. I weigh two hundred and fifty pounds and I am six feet three and a half inches tall."

He replied, "Well, that is good. Don't you think you are big enough to stop that whistling?"

I said, "Oh, yes," in a voice of deep humility. "Mr. Prime Minister, the whistling shall be stopped."

That ended the whistling, but when the Secret Serv ice were changing their posts of duty they would very often exchange a few words of conversation. Then you would hear the British Lion roar, "Stop that talking!"

There was a constant tour of couriers and often they would be invited for meals. The President and the

Prime Minister had code names. A call over the phone would be "Mr. Worthington is calling Mr. Effing ham." I was never too sure who was who, for I failed to note which in my diary.

The Prime Minister was one who was always late to bed, yet he wasn't a late riser. However, he usually took a nap in the afternoon before dinner. It was a pleasure to plan for the comfort of this great man because, like all great men so taken up with the problems of their countries and the world, he showed appreciation for the efforts of those paid to plan the things that were comforting to him.

The Prime Minister was in Florida incognito, so the daily routine was that after dinner he would retire to the library with Mr. Martin, his secretary, Commander Brown, the naval aide, and Sir Charles Wil son, his physician. There they would discuss the problems of the world and as he pranced up and down across the floor, creating phrases, he sometimes would stop and say, "Now there, let's say that again. Yes, put that down. We can use that sometimes, I am sure. Yes, I like that," and he would repeat the phrase. I am sure many of the phrases that always gave a Churchill speech a punch line were created in this manner.

During these sessions Scotch would evaporate. I recall one such night when I thought we had the Prime Minister well-fortified for the nightly session and was near retiring when I was summoned to the library. As I entered, I suppose my face must have reflected my astonishment to see the empty bottles, for the Prime Minister said, "Yes, my man, I need a little more to drink. You see, I have a war to fight and I need fortitude for the battle. And there is one more favor I hope you will do for me."

"Yes, sir," I answered.

"Well," he said, "I hope you will come to my defense if someday someone should claim that I am a teetotaler."

I smiled and said, "Mr. Prime Minister, have no fear, sir. You can depend on me to defend you against such a claim."

He chuckled and said, "That will be all. Good night!"

Mrs. Campbell's cottage was about 1oo feet from the beach, so one fine morning the Prime Minister went for a swim. The beach had usually been cleared. The nearest house was at least three or four blocks away and when the P.M. went in, the Secret Service could not find anyone within a mile of the beach. However, when he had finished his swim there was discovered a woman with a dog strolling on the beach nearby and she sort of loitered around.

As the P.M. was incognito, the Secret Service dared not in any way attract attention to him, so he had to stay in the water, for he was without bathing trunks. We all had a few chuckles concerning his predicament, and of course the P.M. never dared to swim in the raw again.

The afternoon of the day before we left, Harry Hopkins called from Washington and told the Prime Minister not to let me forget to have stone crabs for him before we left. Stone crabs are a delicacy in Florida, and the President and Mr. Hopkins were very fond of them.

So at dinner that night we had stone crabs for an entree. The Prime Minister said he enjoyed them, but he was anxious to know if there was going to be any soup. He said to please an Englishman, soup must always be served.

Mr. Churchill had invited the Prime Minister of Australia to board the train at Jacksonville, Florida, and to dine with him in his stateroom. The dining car waiters brought the food to me in a room next to the stateroom, since the P.M. was still traveling incognito and not even the train crew knew who was in the private car. The entire train crew were curious about their special passenger. One of the vice-presidents of the railroad made the trip and kept the conductor and other train-crew members from interfering with the Secret Service detail and our party. The dining-car waiters thought we were all FBI men. The dining car was kept open for our party after the car had been closed to the travelers. We all ate in the dining car except the Prime Minister. All his meals were served in his stateroom.

The Prime Minister left the train just before we entered the tunnel to cross from Virginia into the District of Columbia. We continued into the capital, where a detail of Secret Service met us. Not until then did our families know where we had been. We returned, as we had left, without any warning.

The end of the Florida trip certainly did not mean that Mr. Churchill's visit was over. He remained with us for nearly a month and a half—from Decem ber, 1941, until nearly February, 1942. He returned again and on September 8, 1943, when Italy surrendered, he was with us. The President had a private luncheon to celebrate the surrender. The guests were Mr. Churchill; Mr. Stimson, the Secretary of War; Mr. Martin, secretary to the Prime Minister; Commander Thompson; Mr. Bernard Baruch, and Colonel Llewellyn.

The party had a ring of joy, but there was also a ring of soberness, for the P.M. remarked, "We are rid of the jackal. Now we can give our full attention to the Hun without this jackal snapping at our heels."

We were getting well acquainted with the Prime Minister of England and he always left something to talk about each time he came and went. The last time I had the honor to prepare for his comfort and entertainment was after the war when he visited this country in 1952 and President Truman gave a luncheon on January 5. The guest list included the British ambassador, Mr. Franks, Anthony Eden, Lord Ismay, Vice President Barkley, Secretary Acheson, Secretary Snyder, Secretary Lovett, General Omar Bradley, Admiral Leahy and several others.

Mrs. Truman was away at the time, so the menus were sent to the President. Whereupon I received this note from President Truman:

"Fields: I made some checks on these menus. I believe that filet mignon would be the best meat course. The Prime Minister is fond of champagne. My salad preference is on No. 1 although No. 3 is excellent. Dessert on No. 1 is best and purely U.S.A., as is the filet. You look all three menus over and we will talk about it. HST."

So from the three menus we decided on oyster soup, celery hearts, assorted olives, filet mignon smothered with mushrooms, watermelon pickles, asparagus hollandaise, grilled tomatoes, hard rolls, hearts-of-lettuce salad and Roquefort dressing, strawberry short cake.

The Prime Minister was in rare form, and on this occasion the habit of drinking was mentioned. He re marked that when he first went to India the drinking water was unfit for human consumption and the only drink fit for humans was whiskey. For that reason he took up the habit of drinking and he just hadn't been able to drop it.

This brought quite a chuckle from the other guests. You would have to see the gestures of the P.M. and hear the inflections of his voice to be able to appreciate his remarks. Without a doubt, Sir Winston Churchill was one of the most impressive, dramatic and dynamic men it has been my pleasure to serve among all the leaders of this era.

Sandwiched in between Sir Winston's visits we had
Mme. Chiang Kai-shek. She was and is a most charming lady to those who did not serve her. She is a proud
and vain lady, especially about her ancestral line, and
her table conversations were mostly about this ancestral
line.

Of course I must say she had encouragement from
the Roosevelts, for the President enjoyed talking about
his ancestors too. But somehow the Roosevelts did not
wear it on their sleeves.

Mme. Chiang was a very light eater—usually very
weak China tea, soups and stewed fruits. A difficult person, extremely nervous and irritable with servants; but
to many of the servants she made up for her demands,
as she was a liberal tipper. Her bed had to be changed
from top to bottom each time she got up. Even if she
went to bed for only ten or fifteen minutes four and five
times a day, each time the bed had to be stripped and
the silk sheets replaced with fresh ones.

She had as her bodyguard a Mr. Kung, her nephew,
and as her traveling companion a niece, Miss Kung.
Miss Kung was not too pleased with the quarters as
signed her at the White House. I understand that she
expressed her objections to the State Department and
after one or two nights she was provided with a suite at
the Mayflower Hotel.

Mme. Chiang, without a doubt, had great charm
and a striking personality, and when she spoke before
the joint Houses of Congress, I heard many of the

gentlemen praise her very much. She departed from her last visit at the White House May 5, 1943. I repeat that Mme. Chiang was a lady with a very im pressive capacity to sway people. Any opinion of the Great Lady of China, however, depended on what status of life the observer might happen to belong to.

Chapter 11

MR. MOLOTOV VISITS
THE WHITE HOUSE

*O*N MAY 29, 1942, I was summoned again to prepare for an off-the-record guest of importance. As with most of the unannounced guests, he would arrive late in the day in time for dinner. The party staying at the White House would be small. The dinner also would be small, in the private dining room and very informal. So I pondered as I prepared my details just whom to expect.

The guests were rushed in through the south grounds and upstairs to their quarters. I did not see them upon their arrival, but shortly afterward I was summoned to the Rose Room. My assignment chart registered a "Mr. Brown" in that room.

A knock at the door was answered by a small, thin man. He spoke excellent English, with an accent that I thought was Swedish. As I glanced over his head into the room I saw near the fireplace a man whom I readily recognized as Mr. Molotov of Russia.

The gentleman at the door was Mr. Molotov's secretary. He asked me to bring Mr. Molotov's valet to him. My chart showed that "Mr. Brown's" valet had the Yellow Room, so I proceeded to the Yellow Room and knocked on the door.

For some time there was no answer. I added a little weight to my knocking and shortly the door opened. For a second I was speechless, for standing before me was a nude woman with a bath towel wrapped—of all places—around her head. She could not speak English and the only words I could say in Russian were "Good morning," but I doubt very much that I could have thought of even those words just then.

I had nothing to say, but she said, *"Ya."*

I said, "Mr. Molotov wants his valet," and she repeated *"Ya."*

I repeated, "Mr. Molotov wants his valet." Again she said *"Ya"* and pushed back into the room, leaving the door open. I turned my back and stepped away from the door and shortly she had a robe on, still with the towel around her head, and I led her to Mr. Molotov's room. I would like to think that I acted just as nonchalant as she did, for she certainly was not at all disturbed as she kept saying *"Ya"* while I tried to tell her my mission.

Mr. Molotov, with his round, chubby face, his stubby mustache and his eyes behind glasses, had an owlish, wise look, especially during conversations when he was listening. At other times his eyes would dart around with the glint of a fox waiting to spring on his prey. It was this that often gave me the idea that perhaps he understood English.

Dinner in the small dining room was served to the President, Mr. Hopkins, Mr. Molotov, his secretary, and Mr. Charles Bohlen, from the State Department, who acted as the interpreter for the President. Mr. Molotov's secretary did most of the talking in English and in Russian and Mr. Bohlen kept the President informed of what was going on. Mr. Molotov's rebuttals were just a little too fast for me and, with the maneuvers of his eyes while a presidential statement was being made, he seemed to be smiling to himself as if he knew what he was going to say before the translations were even started. The President found it necessary to take his time in digesting the full contents of Mr. Molotov's statements during these translations.

Dinner was a simple affair of shrimp cocktails, clear soup, roast saddle of lamb with mint sauce, hearts of lettuce with Russian dressing, and apple pie with sharp cheese.

Mr. Molotov made no particular requests about food or drinks while he stayed with us. He remained only a few days and then moved across the street to Blair House for three or four more. He used to walk, unaccompanied, up and down Pennsylvania Avenue and bought peanuts from Nick, the popcorn man, whose stand was a familiar sight to sightseers and White House occupants for years.

After he returned to Russia his visit was announced to the American public. The man from Russia who many at the time thought might be Stalin's successor seemed to me to be more mystic than impressive. The mystic has no appeal for me. I rather distrust mystic tendencies. By mystic I mean that he seemed to be disinterested in what was being said or what was going on around him. He had so many cards up his sleeve that he was prepared for everything and knew just what move he was going to make.

President Benes of Czechoslovakia arrived on May 13, 1943, for a dinner party and conferences and was a White House guest in addition to Mr. Churchill, who had arrived two days before. President Benes was a very quiet little man and a pleasant personality. He gave the impression of a school professor who was not quite rough enough for the task before him.

I have chosen a few highlights from the many foreign personalities entertained at the White House during these years. By this time these affairs had become so frequent that they were more or less daily routine. I should like to list others whose visits I cannot mention specifically: the King of Greece; the King of Yugoslavia; the King of Iraq; the Duke and Duchess of Windsor; Queen Wilhelmina of the Netherlands; Queen Juliana and Prince Bernhard of the Nether lands; the Duchess of Luxembourg and consort; the Crown Princess and Prince Olaf of Norway; General de Gaulle and General Pétain of France; General Smuts of South Africa; the Duke of Kent; Pandit Nehru of India; Ramsay Mac-Donald; Ernest Bevin; Clement Attlee; Anthony Eden and Lord Mountbatten.

The rigors of the war in late 1943 were beginning to tell on President Roosevelt. The anxieties, long and late hours of conference on war policies, internal policies and politics were taking their toll. He no longer would stand in a receiving line. He remained seated and received guests in a chair to conserve his strength.

Chapter 12

BACK-DOOR POLITICS

*T*HIS book would be incomplete if I did not say something about the White House back-door politics. The household servants were constantly in a dither about the long hours they had to put in and no one would dare to say too much about it. When the Hoovers were in the White House it was a short day for the dining-room and kitchen help if they were through after twelve hours, but they did get one day off a week. The maids, housemen and doormen had much better hours. Despite the pride that existed in those days of a butler feeling his class was above a houseman, most of the men on the butlers' staff—except the head and second man—always welcomed the chance of being detailed to houseman duty because it meant they would get home earlier.

The tension in the dining room under the Hoovers was hard to get used to, I confess. In order to pass the scrutiny of Mrs. Hoover, a servant had to be tops. For her the slightest error was an offense. I do not believe it really mattered too much to President Hoover, but this I will say: anyone who had once served under Mrs. Hoover really knew the formalities of service.

During the Hoover Administration the sounding of three bells would send the help hurrying and scurrying for a hiding place. One of the ushers would rush down the stairs with a doorman who would get the elevator and lock it, waiting for the arrival of the President, and the usher would see that no one was in the corridor.

There was only one elevator then, and anyone on it other than the First Lady, had to jump off as soon as possible. On the second floor, which is the living quarters, there was a closet with a sink near the stair way used by the housemen and maids for their cleaning equipment. If either the President or First Lady came out of their rooms into the corridor the maids, housemen and butlers would scamper to this closet. They would almost run one another down trying to be first in the closet and out of sight, for if they lingered and were seen they would be warned not to let this happen again.

I am sure the President and Mrs. Hoover never requested such actions, but those in charge preferred to have things done this way. It was really funny to see the help packing into that closet. It was like a cat coming into a room and surprising the mice playing. In those days I, too, pushed my way in, and no question about its being full after I got in!

On the roof of the house was a sun parlor which was used as an office for Mrs. Hoover's secretaries, Mrs. Butler, Mrs. McMullin and Miss Hobby. The secretaries usually had luncheon served upstairs in this office at 12:45. The family had lunch at 1 P.M. The butlers' staff at that time consisted of six men—the first, second and third man and the rest of the crew who really did the work, as the song goes. We toted the trays, washed the dishes, cleaned the silver. We had no status except to do what we were told by the three men of rank. So a free elevator during the mealtime meant a lot to the three of us, since we had to carry those trays from the kitchen to the top of the house.

But at 12:45 the elevator would be locked, waiting for the three bells that would signal the coming of the President. Sometimes the doorman might take a chance and run us up, but if he did and the warning bells were to ring, he would be in bad with the head usher, even if he got back before the President arrived.

The top-salaried servants were the valet, head cook and head butler. The rest of us received from $60 to $90 a month and, with the depression on, we were mighty thankful to have a job, for we well knew it could have been worse. Much worse. If you were a butler or cook, you received three meals a day. Other servants, except those that lived in, had two meals a day.

March 4, 1933, brought some changes for the help that were improvements and some that made things worse. They no longer had to run and hide when they heard the President's three bells, and when they were working in the halls, if Mrs. Roosevelt or the President came out, they were told to keep on working. If any of us happened to be near an elevator with a tray and the President or Mrs. Roosevelt was going up, they would call for us to come and ride up with them.

Although the removal of this tension was a great relief and many of the rigid formalities were dispensed with, we had longer working hours and less time off. But the closeness of the family had a way of making us enjoy working hard, up to a certain point.

The first thing Mrs. Roosevelt said was that our days off would be after the serving of lunch once a week, with every other Sunday off after the Sunday midday meal. Vacations would consist of only two weeks.

We soon found out that the day off after lunch meant we would hardly get out before 3:30 P.M., so that the day was gone. On Sundays it was even later. James Mingo and James Reynolds, the two butlers the Roosevelts had brought to the White House, were very disappointed over the working conditions. James Reynolds said he did not think it would do much good to talk to Mrs. Roosevelt about the long hours and inadequate time off. He said this was her custom and she would be hard to convince otherwise. But Mingo started a campaign with Mrs. Dall, and before too long a time we started getting our full day off again. Except me—I had to take whatever day there was when there might not be many activities scheduled, and such days were few and far between. Also, we finally got our full vacation time back.

The next feature which upset the help was the cutting of salaries. The President in his campaign had promised to cut the government cost 25 percent. All salaries were reduced 25 percent, so a check that had read $43.65 the first and fifteenth now read $32.54. The valet, head cook, housekeeper and head butler's salaries were cut at the base pay and then the 25 percent cut. The valet's salary was cut from $150 a month to $75.

The old White House servants were alarmed at the lack of dignity of the valet who appeared in a white coat where all other valets had worn striped pants and short coat in the morning and in the afternoon striped pants and a cutaway coat. McDuffie wore a white coat and most any color pants and shirt and tie. The two butlers had never worn full-dress clothes.

Of course as the chief butler I lowered the dignity of that position, for I did not take walks up Connecticut Avenue in the afternoon in a cutaway coat and striped pants. Also, I broke down the class in the ranks of butlers because we all pitched in and worked together. There was too much work for even the head man to stand around and pose.

In the mornings until after lunch the butlers wore tuxedos, stiff shirts and black ties. For afternoon tea and dinner they wore tails, stiff shirts and white ties both summer and winter. Again the back-door politics changed this to soft shirts with tuxedos and in the summer a light worsted business suit with black tie and soft shirt.

This was much cooler and less expensive, for we had to pay for our laundry and in the Washington heat a stiff shirt and collar didn't last long. With the cuts in salary, we finally got it settled for the laundry to be paid for by the Government.

The Roosevelt grandchildren and nurses added many problems to the duties of serving meals on trays. Finally a kitchen was built on the third floor which also served as a diet kitchen for the President. When all the grandchildren were present, meals could be prepared there and served in the sun parlor or hall.

My wife, Edna, was hired by Mrs. Nesbitt to cook for the grandchildren. I protested, for as I told her, my wife was not a cook. Nevertheless, she went to work and I must say she surprised me, for she certainly cooked much better for them than she had for me. My wife still tells me off about the time I told the people at the White House she couldn't cook. I am not sure whether she has forgiven me, but she certainly hasn't forgotten about it.

She happened to cook a few meals for the President when the grandchildren were there, so now I dare not go into the kitchen at home when a meal is being prepared.

It was during one of these occasions that she had an experience with little Buzzie Dall. He peeped into the kitchen and asked if he might ask her a question. She told him to come in. He climbed up on a kitchen stool, crossed his legs and looked at her for a second or two. Finally he said, "What I want to know is do little boys have to have two daddies?"

I have always admired my wife's ability and at the same time begrudged it because I have never been able to keep up with her retorts. But she said this was one time she had to think before talking. She answered him, "I should think a little boy would be very lucky to have two daddies loving him. Just think how wonderful it is to have one daddy loving you. Some little boys are not lucky enough to have even one daddy to love them."

By this time the other children were calling him to play and she was relieved that the conversation was over.

One of the dearest and just about the most lonesome child ever to live in the White House was Diana Hopkins before her father married again after the death of her mother. She was a well-behaved and very companionable child. Mrs. Roosevelt was busy and likewise Diana's father. The maids were kind to her, but they offered little understanding or companion ship.

She went to a private school and the little Soong girl from the Chinese embassy seemed to be her closest companion. She would go to the Chinese embassy to dinner and the Soong child would come to the White House.

One day a butler, Bill Coates, said to me that Diana and the little girl friend wanted to learn to cook. I said, "When we are not busy they can come in and we will be glad to teach them to make cookies, biscuits and cakes."

Diana was so pleased that she wanted to fix her own lunches for school and we taught her how to set up a tray and a table. She wanted me to put her name on the butlers' weekly schedule, so I made out a schedule with detail for her. She took it seriously and was just as punctual as any member of the crew and she was so pleased with herself for being a part of the crew.

Chapter 13

DEATH OF A PRESIDENT

*D*ESPITE all the problems of the war, a presidential election was looming. It was obvious to those near the President and in position to observe the steady decline in his appearance that the talk of a fourth term would arouse a question as to his ability to see it to the end. He would appear fresh and pink when he arrived at a dinner party, but by the end of dinner he would seem to sag. His face would turn pasty and blanched. Whereas two or three hours prior he had looked alert and pert, he appeared tired and exhausted.

At a luncheon of a few political leaders and members of the family including Mrs. Roosevelt (although the President was not present), the talk was of the need for him to run again. Mrs. Roosevelt made no comments, but Mr. James, who was home on furlough, was very much set against it. He said, "If Father runs for a fourth term and is elected, it will be the means of killing him."

Well, the pros and cons kept this up until the spring of 1944, with the doctors declaring that the President was as good as ever. At that time it was conceded that no doubt the President had a job to finish and only he could see it through.

After the election and Christmas holidays, normal activities continued, but the President had fewer social obligations. To save him from physical wear, the inaugural ceremonies were held on the south portico of the White House. By now the inaugural parties gave me little excitement. However, when one was over and I was complimented it made me feel that I had accomplished something.

The inaugural climaxed three days of teas and dinners, with the house filled with guests. On January 23 we were having a Cabinet dinner, to be followed by Mrs. Roosevelt's double-header teas. Just around the corner would be the luncheon for the movie stars, the March of Dimes Ball and the President's birthday. So each day taxed our imagination and ability, with the war activities added to the duties of keeping the official family comfortable.

On March 17, 1945, the President and Mrs. Roosevelt celebrated their fortieth wedding anniversary. Princess Juliana was paying an informal visit to the Roosevelts. We had the usual exchange of presents between Mrs. Roosevelt and the President. On March 23 the governor general of Canada, the Earl of Athlone, and Princess Alice arrived for a state affair and there was the usual fanfare and dinner.

There were rumors that the President had had an attack at Hyde Park during his stay there during Holy Week. Easter was on April first. The President returned to Washington after Easter and remained two or three days, then took off for Warm Springs, Georgia. I overheard John Mays, the doorman, saying to Admiral McIntire, "I know it is none of my business, sir, but the President looks very bad to me. Don't you think you should have gone with him?"

The admiral said, "I don't think he will need me. However, if it will make you feel any better, I have assigned the Navy's top man to go with him. I am sure he will come back a different man. Ten or twelve days at Warm Springs will make him feel fit as a fiddle."

The twelfth of April started out like any other day. Mrs. Roosevelt, Colonel and Mrs. Boettiger and little Johnny Boettiger were the only ones in the house. For once Mrs. Roosevelt had no important activities scheduled, and after luncheon I took advantage of the situation and went home, leaving word to call me if I was needed.

On arriving home I found that my wife was out and I thought it would be a good time to wax and polish the floors. I turned on the radio while I was working. I really didn't react when first the announcer said, "Our beloved President, Franklin Delano Roosevelt, passed away at Warm Springs, Georgia, today."

I was stunned. I left my floors half finished, changed my clothes and was rushing out of the house when the phone rang. I said, "Hello . . . Yes, I heard and am on my way."

I took a cab, but the cab could not get any closer than Lafayette Park. Thousands of people were packed in the street on the park side across from the White House. Police details were keeping the people on one side of the street. I had to present my I.D. card to cross over to the house.

When I arrived the family was upstairs in the West Hall. I went up and offered my condolences and any service I might be able to render. Though most of us in the house had known that perhaps this might happen, somehow we found it difficult to accept.

This was Thursday afternoon, April 12. Vice-President Truman was sworn in as President of the United States. He called on Mrs. Roosevelt after the swearing in, with Mrs. Truman and Miss Margaret. I was in the West Hall when they arrived.

One of the first things Mrs. Roosevelt said was, "We will be getting out as soon as possible."

President Truman told her, "Now don't you give that a thought. Take your time and do not hurry."

President Truman and his family moved from their apartment to Blair House and doormen and ushers were sent across to Blair House.

Preparations were made to receive the body of President Roosevelt to lie in state in the East Room. The funeral train left for Hyde Park Saturday night. Aboard the train were President Truman, Mrs. Truman, Miss Margaret, members of the Cabinet, Supreme Court justices, political leaders, the press and radio people and the Roosevelt family. The members of the household staff were Mrs. Nesbitt, the housekeeper; Arthur Prettyman, the valet; Alice Palmer, Mrs. Roosevelt's Hyde Park cook; John Boardley, chief messenger, and myself.

It was a cool, chilly April day at Hyde Park. I think most of us who were trembling and with voices quavering when we talked were hoping that our neighbors standing near us would assume that the chill in the spring air was the reason for the tenseness and shivering. But they, too, appeared to be having the same trouble.

After the impressive, white-haired vicar had pronounced the benediction and taps had been sounded over the final resting place of the President we dared not even look at our neighbors or try to say a word. We merely took one last look and walked away with eyes straight ahead.

We left for Washington at noon and next day faced the work of taking inventory of the personal effects which the Roosevelt family had accumulated during twelve years in the White House. I had catalogued the personal silverware, pewter and china, so we did not have too much trouble in my department.

Mrs. Roosevelt was anxious to get away and she warmly thanked me for this effort. Within two weeks a farewell reception was held by Mrs. Roosevelt, the children and grandchildren to say good-by to the household and office help and police guard. This, too, left me emotionally limp, as each member of the family would take my hand and say, "Thank you for being so nice to us for all these years."

Once the family had departed, we had to put our attention on making the house ready for President Truman and his family. Again, after twelve years, we were faced with apprehension, wondering what to expect. Would we be able to please the Trumans, and what would they be like?

Chapter 14

PRESIDENT TRUMAN

$\mathcal{T}$HE Trumans moved into the White House in time for the President's birthday, May 8, 1945, and Elizabeth Moore, who was then the head cook, baked a cake for the President. It was rather funny, for the kitchen had never baked a birthday cake in twelve years; for that matter, no hot rolls, doughnuts, coffee cake or breads either. Sometimes they made popovers for breakfast. Otherwise a local bakery supplied all the breads; hot rolls at the White House meant warmed-over bakery rolls.

President Truman was so pleased with his birthday cake that after dinner he wanted to see the cook and personally thank her. But Elizabeth and her crew had cleared out as soon as the cake had been sent up. Next morning I told her, with a long face, that the President had wanted to see her the night before about the cake she had baked.

She said, "Oh, Fields! What happened? What was wrong with it?"

"You baked it," I said. "Don't you know?" Then I pulled up a chair and said, "Girl, take this seat before you faint. The President was so pleased he merely wanted to thank you personally."

She found it harder to believe that the President wanted to thank her than that something was wrong with the cake. So on his way to the office next morning the President did stop by the kitchen and met the whole crew. This was the first time a President had been in the White House kitchen since Coolidge, and he was in and out so much that it was said he was being nosy—just to see that no handouts were being given away. This started the Truman Administration off with a sense of human understanding and appreciation which never waned during the eight years to follow.

The President did not bring a valet, nor did Mrs. Truman, Miss Margaret or Mrs. Truman's mother, Mrs. Wallace bring any personal maids. Vietta Garr, the family cook in Independence, came along. She would sometimes cook special dishes which the family enjoyed—especially Miss Margaret—and more or less attend the three ladies in personal-maid work. Mrs. Truman, as First Lady, never did require a personal maid during her eight years in the White House and she had only one secretary for personal matters—Miss Odum, who often had luncheon with the family.

Mrs. Helm, who had been Mrs. Wilson's social secretary and also Mrs. Roosevelt's remained with the Trumans. Mrs. Helm and Miss Odum would more or less officiate at teas, pouring for the First Lady, especially when there were from 75 to 200 people. Mrs. Helm could pour a cup of tea, keeping up a conversation with a guest who was dead set on a prolonged conversation, give her the tea and then get rid of her and continue the same running conversation with the next guest faster than anyone I have ever seen—without spilling a drop of tea on the tray.

And the ladies would feel so pleased. I have heard them say, "Oh, I had such a lovely conversation with Mrs. Helm while she was pouring my tea. You know, she is the social secretary." That is the art of pouring, without the people realizing that you do not want them to hold up the line. Miss Odum, at the other end of the table pouring coffee, was a very likable person and she learned to pour coffee just as rapidly without being detained by some long-winded conversationalist.

The Trumans were the most punctual people in the White House during my years there. Breakfast was served at eight o'clock, luncheon at one and dinner at seven. When I went to announce dinner I did not have to stand and wait for someone to recognize me before I could say, "Dinner is served."

The old place quieted down so much we couldn't believe it was the same place. The period of mourning was on, so we didn't have any official entertaining and we had a chance to size up the family. The help found the President, Miss Margaret and Mrs. Wallace easy to size up, but Mrs. Truman, with her reserved personality, had most of the help at first watchful of her. It was agreed that this First Lady would not stand for fakers, shirkers or flatterers, and the only way to gain her approval would be by doing our jobs to the best of our ability. This done, we would not want a more understanding person to work for.

The Trumans did not care for elaborate meals. Neither did the Roosevelts; but, unlike the Roosevelts, the Trumans demanded better-cooked food, for Mrs. Truman is a very good cook and she knew and appreciated good cooking.

I had noticed when we served hot rolls that Mrs. Truman would look at the rolls, break one open and then put it aside. At first I thought that perhaps the rolls were not hot. So the next time I took special care to see that they really *were* hot. But again she did the same thing.

So I said to one of the men, "I am sure I know why Mrs. Truman doesn't eat the rolls. She wants rolls fresh from the oven, not warmed-over bakers' rolls."

Well, when I went into the housekeeper's office next morning to talk over menus with her and the cook, I sensed that they were waiting for me. Right off they told me that my boys were letting the rolls get cold before serving them. They wanted to get a small heating unit just to keep the rolls from getting cold. The cook said the bread was always hot when she sent it up and she was not going to be blamed for our carelessness.

I turned to Mrs. Nesbitt and asked, "Do you mean to say that Mrs. Truman has been asking for hot rolls all this time? Well, no wonder she has not been eating the bread. In fact, no one has. Hot bread doesn't mean warmed-over bakery bread. If you people have forgotten how to bake rolls and bread, then you had better learn. The First Lady wants hot bread from the oven, not warmed-over bakery rolls."

From then on the kitchen posed a problem, for they had been too long on one routine and were not very willing to change. Mrs. Nesbitt had much the same attitude. She was talking to me one day about what Mrs. Truman wanted and said, "I just told her that you don't do things that way. I said Mrs. Roosevelt never did things that way."

"What did she say?" I asked.

She replied, "Nothing. She just looked at me. You know I have been told that I must see to it that she keeps things going around here."

"Well," I said, "I hope you know what you are doing. Mrs. Truman must be a very patient woman, for I am sure that, being a woman, you know what it means to have your way of keeping house compared with some other woman's way."

I never really knew what happened and I never asked anyone about it, but it was not very long after our conversation that Mrs. Nesbitt retired.

The small dining room was used by the Trumans, as by the Roosevelts, for all informal affairs. Breakfast and lunch usually were served on the roof in the sun parlor which was very cheerful and sunny with a view which was not so gloomy as that of either dining room. In fact, there really isn't any view from the dining rooms.

For breakfast the President usually had oatmeal with brown sugar. He always ate whole-wheat toast with his oatmeal and drank about half a cup of coffee. Most likely he would take a piece of ice from his glass of water and drop it into the coffee to cool it.

We had to learn to make coffee for the Trumans. The coffee was brewed in the pantry and, although I never drank coffee myself, each morning I would supervise the brewing of the coffee, trying to find a recipe that would satisfy the Truman taste. I had noticed that Mrs. Truman always took some coffee in the spoon and looked at it before drinking it. I would hover near to view the color of the coffee in the silver spoon when she complained and when she said the coffee was fine. Once I found the color in the spoon that pleased her, we made it that way consistently. In fact, we were so successful that I was sent on a tour of the mess on the presidential yacht to instruct them in the brewing of coffee to please the Truman taste. Shortly after the family moved into the White House the President's brother, Mr. Vivian Truman, came to visit. The first time he appeared in the dining room the President, before he took his seat, said, "Fields, this is my brother, Mr. Vivian Truman."

This was something new for a President to acquaint a member of his family with servants. We were soon to meet all the Wallaces and Trumans in this manner. The President and Mrs. Truman knew each servant by name and at any time a new man was taken into the dining room I would go along and say to the President and Mrs. Truman, "This is —— We are trying him out as a butler."

The President, if seated, would rise and shake hands and say, "Now don't be disturbed by me. You just do what Fields tells you and I know we will be glad to have you aboard." This would at once relieve the tension that faces any waiter or butler who had never been in the presence of the President before. I have seen experienced men who would be so nervous on first going into the White House dining room that you would almost expect them to run up the wall if the President was to say something to them.

The President's mother and sister paid a visit shortly after Mr. Vivian. I don't think the country will forget Mother Truman's statement when she told the press, "I cannot really be glad that my son is President because I am sorry that President Roosevelt is dead." These may not be the exact words, but it went something like that.

And when she arrived by plane with the President and saw the crowds and the press snap ping pictures she said, "Fiddlesticks. If you had told me all this would happen, I would have stayed at home."

For her age, she was most charming and refreshing. She would not have anything to do with the Lincoln Room and they could not get her to sleep in the big bed in the Rose Room with the canopy over it. She preferred the small Rose Room with the small, single bed. She had something friendly to say to any one she came in contact with.

To me the funniest thing she said was one night at dinner with Mr. Joseph Davies, the former ambassador to Russia. During the conversation between the President and the former ambassador a name was mentioned which attracted Mother Truman's interest. She remarked, "Isn't he a Yankee?"

Miss Mary Jane Truman, the President's sister, said, "Now, Mother—"

"Well, isn't he?" she insisted.

The President spoke up and said, "Yes, Mother, but you know there are good Yankees as well as bad and good Rebels."

Mother Truman retorted, "Well, if there are any good Yankees I haven't seen one yet."

Mr. Davies smiled and the conversation was changed. But that was the way she saw it and she did not mince words. I think that the President must have inherited his open, sincere frankness from his mother. Mother Truman and Mother Wallace were as different as night and day, but they were both fine people.

The first of June Mrs. Truman, Miss Margaret and Mrs. Wallace went home to Independence for the summer. The President was alone for breakfast, lunch and dinner. Seldom did he have a guest, and never did the help have it so easy. We were all working an eighteen-hour day now, which was a break in view of the hours we worked before. When Mrs. Truman was away I always talked to the President about the menus and asked if he expected guests. One morning, after I had shown him the menu, the President asked me about the help getting their annual leave. He said, "Fields, you must see to it that no one loses any time, because it belongs to them." I promised that no one in my outfit would lose time. To think that, with all his new duties as President, he had thoughts for these people when many supervisors act as if they are doing you a favor to grant you your annual leave!

With the European theater of the war closed, General Eisenhower and his staff were invited to a dinner at the White House. We had 126 including the general and the President. Among the staff were two colored master sergeants. We set up a bar for the first time in the East Room and had a cocktail hour before dinner. Dinner was informal with the President and the general seated at the round mahogany table in the center of the State Dining Room with twelve other soldiers. Around the center table were smaller ones and the overflow were seated in the Red Parlor.

When General Eisenhower came in I recalled how, not too many years ago, he was a major. I heard many conversations by General Marshall praising "this fellow Eisenhower"—the term he used in talking to President Roosevelt. There is no doubt in my mind that General Marshall really sold the President on Major Eisenhower. He was always praising him. Later on I was to hear many conversations about "this fellow Eisenhower."

In July, 1945, the President went to Potsdam for a meeting with Churchill and Stalin and I remembered a remark President Roosevelt had made in the late summer of 1944 during the campaign. He said that if the war was over before the election, he and Churchill both were likely to be defeated because the people, being tired of war, would most likely want to change their leaders. While he was in Potsdam, this prediction came true in Churchill's case, and the meeting recessed until the new Prime Minister, Clement Attlee, could join them.

Prime Minister Attlee was with us a few months later in November. It seemed strange to call anyone other than Churchill "Mr. Prime Minister," and Attlee somehow just did not strike the gong like Churchill.

When the ladies returned from Missouri that fall they brought some sorghum molasses. Miss Margaret, especially, was very fond of cornbread and sorghum. From my boyhood in Indiana when sugar cane was cut and carried to the mill, I can still smell the cooking of the syrup into molasses and see a lazy old mule moving just fast enough for the mill to grind the cane into the syrup that was cooking.

Miss Margaret said to me one day as she was leaving the table where they had been talking about molasses and cornbread, "Fields, that is real good eating."

And I agreed with her for, as a kid, we always had a big barrel of molasses sent from the mill. As the winter wore on, the molasses got thicker and thicker, but it never did turn into sugar. That is what makes an expert molasses maker—the art of cooking the syrup so that it would not turn into sugar. With hot biscuits, cornbread or pancakes and butter and a plate of good sorghum molasses, no eating could be better.

The President attended his first Armistice Day services as President on Sunday, November 11, 1945. The Trumans always followed their family tradition of having Sunday dinner at midday and this day we had some of Miss Margaret's favorite dishes, including chocolate ice cream. The President spoke about especially privileged people and said, "Fields, I don't want you boys spoiling my girl." He delighted in teasing Miss Margaret and the First Lady and when he did they could always give him a good going over.

On one occasion when they had been riding him, he said to me as he left the dining room: "Fields, what do you think of that?"

I said, "Mr. President, I am afraid you have the same problem at home that I have."

He said, "What is that?"

"Sir," I said, "a wife and daughter. You cannot win unless you can sow a seed of doubt as to which one is boss."

He laughed and said, "That question was settled years ago."

The President was big enough to boss the country, but to the President Mrs. Truman was the "boss." I have never heard her try to tell him what was good for the country, but one time I did hear her warning him for his own good about a Cabinet officer. I do not recall the exact reasons for her so forewarning him, but it was about Secretary Wallace.

The President replied, "Oh, Henry is all right."

President Truman had so many ways that were cordial and genuine, but only a fool would fail to appreciate this cordial intimacy by being disrespectful.

During the Roosevelt Administration a messenger by the name of John Pye used to prepare lunches for some of the White House secretaries, and during the Truman Administration in the basement under the President's office he really set up a kitchen and dining room for such people as Mr. Charles Ross, Mr. Short, Mr. Hassett, Mr. Matt Connelly, General Graham, General Vaughan and Mr. Clifford. Sometimes Pye would have some of the Cabinet officers as guests, and even the President himself whenever he could manage to get him.

When Mrs. Truman was away sometimes the President would have Mr. Connelly call me and ask what did I think of the President eating in Pye's dining room. Usually I would say that if the doctor was nearby, perhaps it would be all right. Otherwise I would advise the President to come to lunch at the White House where he would be safe and not eat anything that John Pye cooked.

Naturally the President would wait until John Pye was within hearing distance and then relate my advice. John was one of those characters who get upset. He would say, "Indeed, Mr. President, there is nothing wrong with this food! Fields doesn't know what he is talking about. I swear by the Almighty that you are safe here, sir."

Pye was happiest when he could get the President downstairs in the office of his dining room. Sometimes he would invite Miss Margaret and Miss Odum to luncheon and I would blast him to high heaven for trying to take my customers away. The President got fun out of this feud between John Pye and me. Pye and I were the best of friends and we, too, enjoyed the feud.

Chapter 15

CHRISTMAS IN THE WHITE HOUSE

I SHALL always remember the first Truman Christmas in 1945. About a week before, the President said one morning when he was alone at breakfast, "Fields, I should like to request a favor. I want you to find a needy colored family and see to it that they have a real happy Christmas dinner. I have already asked Dressler"—the agent in charge of the Secret Service detail to the President—"to find a needy white family."

The President went on to say that he did not want it known. He took out his purse and gave me some money, saying, "This is to buy each child in the family a present. If this isn't enough, let me know."

I had never had such a detail and decided to call on the Southeast Settlement House, in South Washington. I went that afternoon and talked to the lady in charge. She wanted information about me, why I came and my object and my name. This I wasn't prepared for. I felt that if I gave my name, she might reason who was the donor of the money. All that day I had been humming tunes from *Tales of Hoffman* by Offenbach, so when she asked my name, "Offenbach" came into my head. I changed this and said instead, "Colonel Offendorf."

She seemed a little startled, but "Colonel Offendorf" it was. The social worker gave me the name of a family—a mother with nine children, the eldest a girl of thirteen. The husband had been found murdered three months before. He had no family, nor did the mother. The Settlement had just learned about this family and was happy to have me help them.

I said I would like to go and meet the mother and see the situation. What I saw was beyond my imagination. Within sight of the Capitol, this was poverty of the worst sort, and the mother little realized that she could get help from any source. I do not believe she could read and it was the thirteen-year-old girl who had taken it on herself to appeal to the Settlement House.

When I looked around, the very first thing I discovered was that there was no cooking stove. The woman was cooking on a potbellied heating stove with a pot of beans cooking in clear water. I thought to myself that I was glad I had taken the time to investigate. What a cruel joke it would have been to send this family a thirty-pound turkey with no place to cook it.

So when I reported to the President my findings I said that there was no telling, perhaps the white family might be in the same position. So I would have both turkeys stuffed and cooked in the White House kitchen. From then on each Thanksgiving and Christmas the chief of Secret Service detail and I selected families in need for these gifts from the President. The deliveries were always made in private cars and this is the first time I have told this story.

Christmas in the White House during the Roosevelt and Truman administrations was always a friendly, family occasion. Christmas with the Hoovers had been a time of cordial but reserved master-to-servant-like greetings. President and Mrs. Hoover would come into the East Room and say "Merry Christmas" to all the household staff gathered around the big tree in that room. Gifts would be passed out—an autographed picture and an envelope with a crisp new $5 bill for servants of the lower bracket, and larger amounts for those of the higher brackets. Then President and Mrs. Hoover would bow and leave and there would be no hand shaking.

During the Roosevelt Administration all the servants and their entire families would gather downstairs in the corridor and, just as for formal receptions, they would proceed to the East Room to be introduced by an aide to the President, the First Lady and other members of the family.

A list of the children under sixteen in each family had been made months before and each child received a gift as well as the opportunity to shake hands with the

President and First Lady—a memorable thing for any child.

The Trumans continued this policy, and I understand that the Eisenhowers carried on this family-like gathering for the office workers and servants. It is true that the Trumans celebrated Christmas in the White House only twice because Mrs. Truman, Miss Margaret and Mrs. Truman's mother, Mrs. Wallace, always left for Missouri a few days before Christmas. But the President always remained for the White House Christmas party.

The times when the Trumans were at the White House for Christmas Mrs. Truman scheduled the family dinner at 2 P.M. and all the help was released to spend the rest of the day with their own families. Sandwiches and the makings had been prepared, and the Trumans enjoyed getting things for themselves. I am sure they felt more at home than if they had had servants fussing around them, and the White House help certainly did appreciate the opportunity of spending a part of Christmas Day at home with their families. At least I did, and I know many others did likewise.

The Roosevelts always had Christmas at the White House with all the children and most of the grandchildren there. They always braved the hazards of fire by having a Christmas tree lighted with candles in the East Hall. The family tradition included reading of Charles Dickens' *Christmas Carol* by the President. The gathering of the family with the President and Mrs. Roosevelt, the President's mother, the children and grandchildren made a comely family group of four generations.

There were many other traditions in this family which showed such zest for enjoying themselves with life's activities. The holidays were for fun, and, as a real family, they had fun.

The Christmas dinner was at eight o'clock and usually there was a movie after dinner, then refreshments. We could all join in and watch the movies, but it was not like being in your own humble abode with your own family.

President Truman usually had Cabinet luncheons whenever the Cabinet met. In the Hoover and Roosevelt administrations I never really got acquainted with the Cabinet members, though I served them very often—except for some few friendly men like Secretary Stettinius and Secretary Hull. These gentlemen would always speak, no matter where they saw me.

Secretary Stettinius met me in the corridor one night at a party. With him were Mrs. Stettinius and Mr. and Mrs. Nelson Rockefeller. He stopped and said to his guests, "I want you to meet a good friend of mine." From then on Mr. Rockefeller, a most friendly gentleman, always spoke to me and would chat. I saw him often during the Roosevelt Administration. One night during the Truman Administration, after I had not seen him for some time, he was a dinner guest and he left the line entering the dining room to shake my hand.

In the Truman Administration, because of the friendliness of the President, the Cabinet officers followed the cue. One time when I was sending my wife to Boston to the Lahey Clinic we had to wheel her to the train in a chair. I helped her get a bed, and a nurse who was a devoted friend was to meet her in Boston. After getting my wife fixed up for the trip I was leaving her bedroom when I almost bumped into Secretary Snyder and Secretary Forrestal and their wives.

Secretary Snyder said, "Well, look who is here. Fields, what are you doing?"

I explained my mission and both ladies said, "If you like we will be glad to look in on your wife during the trip." These are the acts of kindness that fill one with faith that God watches and does touch the hearts of people in high and low places.

The year 1947 brought many people into my life who were moved to help my wife and me out of our worst difficulties during the eleven years of her ill health. We had friends in Wellesley, Massachusetts, and without their looking out for her while I was working in Washington, I am sure my wife would not have survived to be blessed to see and enjoy our two granddaughters, now eleven and six, the children of our daughter, Virginia, and son-in-law, Stanley Yancey.

In July, with my wife's condition still critical, my mother passed away in Indianapolis. I received the information at five o'clock in the morning and around seven called the White House to say that I would go to

Indianapolis that day. Around nine o'clock a White House usher phoned and said that the President had arranged a flight and that a White House car would pick me up and take me to Andrus Field.

I arrived in Indianapolis at five in the afternoon. The next day flowers arrived from the White House. In about ten minutes a newspaper called and wanted to know how did Mrs. Fields know President Truman and could they come and get a picture? I told them definitely no.

The Indianapolis papers had the information of the wreath from the President on their front pages. Mother was being waked at the house. My brother George and I were invited out for dinner that night and when we returned home we were startled, for we had a front yard full of people. Of course Mother had always been a ward and precinct political worker and at the time of her death she had a political job at the statehouse.

Politically Mother and Father separated during the election of 1936. Dad was the G.O.P. ward leader and mother was the Democratic women's leader, and Mother always licked dad in the elections. They had a truce at home; no politics were permitted there. But once they left the house, no holds were barred and the community enjoyed their rivalry. Of course with Mother being with the winners, she had been able to deliver a few favors to the community.

In late September I went to Wellesley and brought my wife back to Washington. She was helpless, but she wanted to come home. She could hardly sit up and every effort was filled with pain. Edna has remarkable courage and patience. Through all the years of her illness she never felt sorry for herself. Her unflagging determination gave me hope when the doctors could hardly give me any. Today, after twelve years, she still has this same determination.

Christmas of 1947 found Mrs. Truman's brothers, Frank, George and Fred Wallace, and their wives at the White House, and also Mr. Fred's children, David and Marian. Miss Mary Truman, the President's sister, was among those present. Even at Christmas the Trumans' entertaining was never as hilarious as the Roosevelts', because of the lack of children and grandchildren. For Christmas dinner we had only the family of twelve, whereas the Roosevelts would have had that many grandchildren alone.

Dinner was in the small dining room at 2 P.M. and Miss Margaret snapped pictures of the family group and the butlers. We all got pictures of the party and I am mighty proud of mine. It was one of the few times that President Truman ever carved at the table.

With dinner at 2 P.M., Mrs. Truman had asked to have the third floor kitchen supplied with the makings of sandwiches for supper so that the help could take the rest of the day off. While the Trumans were in the White House the third-floor kitchen was always supplied with the makings of sandwiches for late snacks for Miss Margaret and her two chums, Miss Lingo and

Miss Snyder. In the big White House kitchen we kept the refrigerators locked because, somehow or other, the spirits that roamed at night were usually hungry and thirsty. It could not have been the servants, for most of them went home nights, so that left, besides the family, the police detail and Secret Service detail. At least the spirits did not have the ability to go through locked doors or to unlock them, and with both security details to watch the locked doors we could always find things safe.

Chapter 16

THE ELECTION OF 1948

*T*HE year 1948 brought us into another presidential campaign. There were some rumblings after the President went before Congress and presented his ten-point civil-rights program. But in July, after Alabama and Mississippi walked out of the convention because of the civil-rights plank, President Truman made his acceptance speech. Mrs. Truman and Miss Margaret went to Philadelphia to be with him.

The next morning, after a short night's sleep, I went to work. There wasn't any information about breakfast. I knew that the train did not leave Philadelphia until nearly 4 A.M. and I was sure that Mrs. Truman, Miss Margaret and Mrs. Wallace would not have breakfast at 8 A.M. But, despite his retiring late, I was not too sure about the President. When I learned that he did not get to bed until his usual arising time, 6 A.M., I told the boys in the pantry and kitchen that I would take a stroll down to the second floor about 9 o'clock to see if the President was stirring.

So about 9:15 I saw a light in the study. As I eased the door open to peep inside the President laughed and said, "Good morning, Fields."

I said, "Good morning, Mr. President. We did not hear from you and I was nosing around to see if you were up."

"Yes," he replied. "I am the only one up. The women-folks will be calling you later, and you can send me a tray up here when it is ready."

I said, "Sir, you had a rough night."

"Yes, I did," he replied, "but, Fields, I am going to win this thing if there is a God in heaven."

I replied, "Yes, sir. With God's help you will win."

The next day the President called an extra session of Congress, and during the campaign he went out and met people to tell them why he had to call the members back. All of us who knew him felt that the more people he met with his off-the-cuff, friendly talks, the more they would believe in his sincerity. So the President went on what they called "whistle stops."

In the early part of August it was found that the second-floor Lincoln bedroom that Miss Margaret used as her sitting room was sinking down to the small dining room. Mr. Winslow, the White House architect and engineer, started investigating and it was thought that steel rods fastened to the beams from the reinforced steel-and-concrete third floor would sort of hold the floor in suspension.

The President said at a press conference that he was sitting at his desk in the study when the butler brought his tray and he felt the whole floor sway as if floating in space. So he called the White House architect and it was found that the second floor was falling down. Well, my old friend, John Pye, had a field day. He called me and said that it was in all the newspapers that I was so big, with my flat feet, that the White House was falling down under my weight.

Before the campaign was over the East Room ceiling started to come down and there was left only one thing to do—tear the old place down and rebuild. It cost over $5,000,000. The campaign had to be fought by the President as the Berlin crisis grew worse, plus the house falling down on him.

During the height of the campaign there was a meeting and dinner of former Democratic national chairmen with the President. They were Flynn, Walker, Barkley and one other man I have forgotten, besides McGrath of Rhode Island, then chairman. Mr. Flynn had just published a book and the conversation turned to certain references to F.D.R. Well, when Messrs. Flynn, Barkley and Walker finished expressing some of their opinions about F.D.R., they certainly left me with a funny feeling and a new appraisal of this great man. But then I reasoned that, like all men, he was human and should be expected to be subject at least to some of the faults of men, such as "egotism," "vindictiveness," "hallucinations of grandeur" and "deceit."

I also felt that these men were wrong to say such things about their leader of the past. However, perhaps their opinions, expressed in confidence, did not mean that they thought any less of him but that they appreciated the moments when he overcame these weaknesses. To deny that he had many of these faults would have made him a saint. And no man can be a political leader and President and at the same time be a saint too.

Well, as the election day drew nearer, it was conceded by most political writers and pollsters that Governor Dewey would be our next President. The only encouragement came from Mr. Biffle, the secretary of the Senate, who had disguised himself as a chicken peddler and gone over the countryside with his polling system. He declared that Truman would be elected.

I had a feeling that perhaps the good Lord was not on the President's side this time, though my wife kept saying that, despite the papers, he was going to win. On the day of the election it was the only topic talked about at the White House. I do not recall when there was ever as much excitement and open discussion as went on around the place during this election. Many were making bets pro and con.

That night I started to keep tally as the news came over the radio. At first the commentators would say that

President Truman was showing a slight lead, but it was the industrial centers which had machine voting and the count was bound to be overcome when the upstate votes were in. Well, the reports got so exciting that it appeared there was going to be an upset. I have forgotten when I went to bed—if I did—content to know that the President had been re-elected.

There was a big victory parade to the White House when the family returned from Independence. Where just four years before President Truman rode in a similar parade as Vice-President-elect, now he was the President and President-elect both. With him was Vice-President-elect Barkley. It was a modest but very happy family and we all were happy for them.

But with the White House falling down, plans had to be made to vacate. There was talk of moving to several other places before the decision was made to move to the Blair house. We had to start packing china, silver, linens and other equipment for storage and to take to Blair house. Most of the White House things which we took were put in the Lee house. A door was cut through on the first floor, the two kitchens had connecting doors and on the top floor you could go from one house to the other. We used the Lee house for teas, luncheons and dinners. The Blair dining room was smaller and the family used that room.

Mrs. Geaney, the housekeeper for the Gist Blairs, remained when the house was turned over to the State Department. She was very proud of some rare old pieces of silver, and there were also choice pieces of Spode, Minton, Dresden, Wedgwood, and Sandwich glass. The old house was filled with historical treasures, including some letters from President Lincoln to the first Mr. Gist Blair, who was the son of Montgomery Blair, who was a member of the Lincoln Cabinet. The quarters where we butlers changed our clothes had been the slave quarters where the servants were locked in at night. The bars were still on the windows.

Though the Blair house was a very old and attractive place, we just would not have room to do any big entertaining there. The dining room on the Lee side could seat only about 22 guests. By combining the two sitting rooms, we could accommodate about 100 people for tea, so we had a lot of small teas. The inaugural luncheon, reception and dinners had to be held elsewhere.

The reception was at the Mellon art gallery. Caterers supplied the service for the guests and we served the President's table. The Wallace and Truman families were house guests and, except for a few personal friends, these two families occupied our time. I took my second man, John Ficklin, to the art gallery to serve the President's table and left Charles Ficklin, the first man, in charge to prepare the dinner that night. My wife and I received an invitation to attend the Inaugural Ball. Of course we were not able to attend, but we have preserved this invitation for our great-grandchildren.

Mrs. Geaney, who had always been in charge of the Blair house, was finding it difficult to get along with the ushers who really manage the White House. I never found out the true story, but by April of 1949 she moved from the Blair house. The head cook, Elizabeth, and her assistant also left. This, too, I never knew the reasons for.

Late in the afternoon of April 27 Mr. Crim, the chief usher, called me to his office and said that President and Mrs. Truman wanted me to take full charge and especially to organize the kitchen and plan all the menus.

Once the kitchen personnel was organized, I started to work out a system to keep track of foods bought and used. No real records had been kept of cost, the amount of food used and the amount remaining. Each month thereafter Mrs. Truman could go over the records and know the actual cost of running the house hold.

During the Roosevelt Administration certain people would call and say, "I have to work late. Can you send me a tray?" Or "I am having two or three people in for lunch." Who was to question their authority? Yet these bills had to be paid by the President, and not out of any state fund. I have heard President Roosevelt say on a number of occasions, "I am not going to have these folks eating on me." Except for official functions, the President has to pay for each guest invited to dine with him. Of course the Trumans were never the type to go out and bring back guests the way the Roosevelts did—especially Mrs. Roosevelt and the children.

Preparing menus for the Trumans was not too easy. Not that they were difficult to please or fussy, but Mrs.

Truman was on a salt-free diet, the President required a low-calorie and high protein diet, and Mrs. Wallace needed all the calories she could get. Miss Margaret was away most of the time, working at her career of singing and the stage. Only when she was home could we go overboard. The family meals were simple three-course affairs except for Sundays or when guests had been invited.

Miss Margaret had a dinner dance and buffet supper in May, 1949, my first of such affairs after taking over full command. Of course we had had teas—many of them—prior to this. At one of these teas Mrs. Roosevelt and Grandma Moses were present. It was the first time Mrs. Roosevelt had been to see us since 1945 and we all were very glad to see her. Grandma Moses asked the President to play the piano for her and seemed so proud when he did. I must say Grandma Moses was without a doubt the darling of that party.

On October 11 we had a state visit from His Excellency, Jawaharlal Nehru, the Prime Minister of India. His sister, Mme. Pandit, was the ambassadress from India. She was one of the most attractive women in the diplomatic world. Prime Minister Nehru had a noble-looking face with wise, mystic eyes. Perhaps his native dress added to that mystic look. He also had a most vibrant, musical voice. On first seeing him, you might expect him to be warm and friendly, but you never found that to be so. Mme. Pandit, however, was a friendly person.

Chapter 17

THE KOREAN WAR

SUNDAY, June 25, 1950, was to me like most of my weekends when the wife was away. Since her last operation she had usually left for Boston and the Lahey Clinic in early April. I really dreaded week ends, especially when the President and the family were away. This was one of Washington's hot June Sundays. I skipped church and did not even bother to shave. Around 4 P.M. my phone started to ring. I lifted the receiver to find that Mr. Claunch, the White House usher, was on the other end.

He said, "Fields, the President is flying back from Independence. He has invited the chiefs of staff, the Secretary of State and some others for dinner tonight. He is due at eight thirty and the guests have been invited for eight o'clock. You are to have cocktails and hors d'oeuvres for them while they are waiting. When he comes they will go right in to dinner."

While he was talking I was planning what to have for dinner and also how many of the help I could round up, for we had let them all off for the weekend. I asked Mr. Claunch to see what he could do in helping me locate a crew through police calls and radio. I was able to locate two cooks and in the cab on my way to the White House I made up a menu.

I gave the menu to the cooks and started to prepare the hors d'oeuvres and set the table. At eight o'clock it appeared as if I might have to serve the dinner myself. Cocktails were being served when three of the butlers arrived. They finished readying the table while I served the cocktails.

There was conversation about the Korean situation and Secretary Johnson asked Secretary Acheson, "How did the President take it when you told him?" The Secretary replied, "He did not hesitate a second. He was positive and all action."

General Omar Bradley and Admiral Sawyer were in a huddle. There was much talk of terrain and air support.

The President arrived at 8:30 and I said, "Good evening, sir. We are ready."

This is how the Korean War started with me.

On Monday we had a Cabinet luncheon and General Bradley brought maps along and the progress of the "police actions," as it was called then, was explained to the Cabinet.

On All Saints' Day, November 1, 1950, at about 2 P.M. I was in the kitchen going over the menus for the next day when suddenly Miss Walker, the assistant housekeeper, rushed in hysterically saying, "They are shooting at each other in the street and White House policeman Downs is in the office bleeding."

I rushed into the office, wondering what the police were doing shooting at one another. I found Officer Downs lying on a couch with wounds in his chest, neck and abdomen. I moved him to a supine position on the floor and asked the chief, Medina, to bring me towels. I had to cut the blood-soaked tie off his neck and attempted to apply pressure bandages to stop the bleeding. I asked the mess attendant from the Navy to get an ambulance. I don't know where Smith and Medina went, but it seemed like ages that I was there alone, trying to aid the wounded officer. He was constantly trying to get up and I was almost forced to hold him down, for he was losing so much blood. Nash, another messenger, heard I was alone with the wounded officer and came to help. Then the ambulance arrived, but the nurse and an attendant were busy picking up a civilian who had been wounded. Later I learned that this man was dead.

By that time a police wagon had pulled up with three officers, and we carried Officer Downs to the patrol wagon. After they drove off to the hospital I learned what had caused all this excitement. Two Puerto Ricans had made an attempt on the President's life by crashing through the front door of the Blair house. White House policemen Birrell and Downs were wounded and White House policeman Coffelt had been slain.

The death of White House policeman Coffelt was almost unbelievable, for I had been talking to him just about twenty minutes before he went on duty.

It was well that the Puerto Ricans did not really lay plans for their attempt on the President's life for, if they had, they might have at least entered the house, which would have made a very nasty situation. The post where White House policeman Coffelt was slain left the Lee side of the house unprotected. Of course the President was on the Blair side, but on the second floor you could easily go from the Lee house into the Blair house.

The President was upstairs taking a nap when the commotion started and, without being aware of his own danger, was watching the action from the front windows. Of course it is hard for a President to believe that anyone would want to harm him, but as soon as he is elected he becomes the target of well-wishers, do-righters, know-allers, faultfinders and crackpots. I understand that this feeling that no one would want to harm him had placed the guards at a handicap. The house is right on the street and anyone could walk right up to the front steps or side entrances without being intercepted unless he started up the steps.

From that time on no sidewalk traffic was permitted on that side of the street and bulletproof glass was installed in the windows.

The funeral service for White House policeman Coffelt was attended by the President, Mrs. Truman, Miss Margaret and the Cabinet officers. I was asked to represent the household help with Mitchell, who was in charge of the presidential train when he went on trips and at other times was on the messenger staff.

I had been caught unprepared and was ashamed of the hat I was wearing. The weather was very cold and I had to walk across the street to reach the car assigned for the service. Otherwise I would not have needed a hat, but I catch cold so easily without one. Mitchell was already in the car and looked so well groomed.

We were sitting together and the car was waiting for someone else. When the other person arrived, it turned out to be Ambassador Harriman. When I saw his hat I felt relieved, for I thought, "If Mr. Harriman with all his money can wear a hat like that, what have I to be ashamed of?"

In late December of 1950 and early January, from bits of conversations I heard from the Cabinet members, the world was again faced by a scare of a third world war. The President was very angry with Prime Minister Attlee. I never understood the full details but

I knew that, though the general public thought all was well, the President and members of the Cabinet were having moments of anxiety.

In January we started a series of teas for veterans in the hospitals and in and around Washington. We would have two and sometimes three a week, and served cider, cola, tea, coffee and real homemade doughnuts, sandwiches, candies and nuts. The President would always attend these affairs. Many Wacs, Waves or G.I.'s would be amazed to turn around and find themselves face to face with the President, saying, "Hello there, how are you? Are they treating you right?" He would enter without an aide's announcing him. President Truman seemed to get a great kick out of chumming with these service people.

I heard a sailor telling a friend how he looked around and there he was, facing the President. He said, "Gee, fellows, I almost lost my voice. Wait till I tell them at home about this. I was kidding and telling them what I was going to say to Harry and they bet me I wouldn't even see him. I know they aren't going to believe this. How can I make them believe me?"

On June 17 Mr. Crim requested me to have a complete setup for a formal tea but no tea for a group of six or eight newspaperwomen. He said, "Mr. West will usher them in and you are to be nearby in case any questions are asked about the china and so forth."

At 10:30 Mr. West ushered the ladies in and they started plying him with questions. I was standing in the background and he called the ladies' attention to me and the questions came my way. I explained about the different chinas, silverwares and linens and was questioned about the gold flatware service used at state dinners.

I explained the history of the service. Then they asked how many complete settings we could provide for. This was my chance, so I told them the story; how we had to wash tablespoons and dessertspoons used for soup and then rush back for another course, that we had no fish forks and knives and no salad forks.

When we had the King and Queen of England in 1939 I had mentioned all this to President Roosevelt, but he said buying gold tableware would be criticized by the politicians. I felt that these ladies might tell the public about this and appeal to the pride of the people of the richest country, as the White House was their house for entertaining the prominent people of the world.

We did finally complete the gold service and, besides that, bought some very much needed china which is called the Truman china. It is Lenox, as are the two other American-made sets of china in the house, the Wilson and F.D.R. china. The Wilson and F.D.R. chinas are blue and gold on a bone-white background. The Truman china is green and gold against the bone-white background. The coat of arms on the Truman china has the eagle looking toward the talon holding the olive branch of peace. The Wilson and F.D.R. chinas show the eagle looking toward the talon holding the arrows which are symbolic of war. This change was also made by President Truman on the presidential flags and seals.

The crowning and most important social event of 1951 was the visit of Princess Elizabeth of England and the Duke of Edinburgh. The royal party arrived at the Blair house late in the afternoon of October 31. They were scheduled to go to a press reception at 5:15, so we did not have a state tea. We had small tea trays for the princess and the duke in their bedrooms and set up tea in the Lee sitting room for the aide, secretary, and lady in waiting. But Her Royal Highness and the duke, instead of having tea in their rooms, joined the others in the sitting room. Dinner was at 8 P.M. for 22 guests; 100 more had been invited to the reception after dinner.

The princess, a very charming, angelic-appearing young woman, was small. Her profile showed her mother's graciousness, while, facing you, she had the eyes and noble expression of her father, King George. The duke, a tall, handsome, blond man with an irrepressible personality, seemed always to be keeping himself in the background—never appearing other than a devoted subject and escort, not as a husband. He walked into the room a pace or two behind the princess. From all appearances, the duke was well equipped to be a consort and companion to the queen and share her glory.

Mrs. Truman selected the following menu for dinner that night:

BLUE POINTS ON HALF SHELL
COCKTAIL SAUCE, LEMON WEDGES
CRACKERS
SHERRY
CLEAR SOUP WITH MARROW BALLS
CELERY HEARTS ASSORTED OLIVES
MELBA TOAST
WHITE WINE
LOBSTER THERMIDOR
PARSLEYED SLICED TOMATOES AND CUCUMBERS
WHOLE-WHEAT-BREAD SANDWICHES
RED WINE
ROAST FILLET BEEF
WINE ESSENCE
WATERMELON PICKLES
BROILED MUSHROOMS
FRENCH FRIED POTATO BALLS
ASPARAGUS HOLLANDAISE
CHAMPAGNE
GREEN SALAD WITH ARTICHOKE HEARTS
BAKED OLD MISSOURI HAM
HERB FRENCH DRESSING
CORN STICKS
VANILLA-ICE-CREAM MELON MOLDS
BRANDIED MACAROONS
ANGEL-FOOD CAKE

Next morning at eight o'clock Princess Elizabeth had a cup of coffee and a glass of orange juice. Breakfast was served to the royal party in the Lee sitting room at nine o'clock. It consisted of melon, orange juice, scrambled eggs, bacon and sausages, toast, hot biscuits and marmalade and tea. The princess had cream in her tea.

Besides Her Royal Highness and the duke, the royal party included Mrs. Andrew Elphin stone, lady in waiting, and Lieutenant Michael Parker, the duke's aide.

I went up to check the service and to announce breakfast. Princess Elizabeth and the others were ready, except for the duke. I seated Her Royal Highness and the others and they had nearly finished their melon when in rushed the duke, saying, "I'm afraid I am a little late."

He was in his shirt sleeves with his collar open and he grabbed a seat before anyone could seat him. The princess did not stop eating her melon, although the others stood while the duke was taking a seat. Seeing the duke there in his shirt sleeves with his collar open gave me the feeling that this was the behavior of a commoner and not what you would expect from royalty. And I admired his audacity, for I know what a blasting I would have got if I had been visiting with my wife and had come out in my shirt sleeves, or even at home when we had guests. It was pleasing to find the duke to be a human being who, no doubt, felt more comfortable in his shirt sleeves when at least one meal could be homelike.

After breakfast the next day we said good-by to H.R.H. Princess Elizabeth, the duke and their royal party. This charming young woman soon was destined to be the ruler of the great British Empire. On this visit we found that the duke's valet and the princess's maid were real nice people without any of the ways that had made problems with the royal servants of the princess's parents, King George and Queen Elizabeth, in 1939. I still regret that I was not able to complete the cycle with Princess Elizabeth after she was crowned queen as I had with Princess Juliana of Holland after she became Queen Juliana.

Chapter 18

THE CAMPAIGN OF 1952

*T*HE Trumans moved back to the newly renovated White House in March of 1952. It had been a tough job putting the old place back into shape. Though there were many fine improvements, the house looked the same. Care had been taken so that everything would be an exact likeness of the original rooms. I suppose the biggest change was in the State Dining Room. The old English oak-paneled walls had been tinted green instead of their original stain. Many of us were apprehensive about this, but once you saw the change it surprised you how much it added to the room. With the new Truman china, the same shade of green and gold, placed on white damask linen it added brightness to this room which is inclined to be dark and somber.

We christened the new dining room with a luncheon for Queen Juliana of the Netherlands. She and

Prince Bernhard were not strangers to us, for during their exile in Canada during the war we had often had them as off-the-record guests. Her Majesty was just as charming as ever and had developed a graciousness and poise suitable to the ruler of a country.

Saturday, April 5, the royal party was scheduled to leave the airport at 9:15. Breakfast was to be served for Her Majesty and the prince in the East Hall at 8:05. Her Majesty's quarters were the Rose Room, and for the prince the Lincoln Room where the Emancipation Proclamation was signed.

The table was in readiness and the queen was on time, but the prince was not ready. I announced breakfast to His Royal Highness and he replied, "Just a minute!" as he poured a short snort of Holland gin.

Shortly he rushed out and the queen, in Dutch, gave him a talking to. She was not smiling and the tone of voice was that of a wife scolding a husband. And like a wise husband, the prince kept quiet. I left the butlers to finish serving and I thought, "Maybe they are queen and prince, but right at that moment they were just plain man and wife." At 8:45 we bade farewell to this delightfully human couple and their royal party.

That afternoon we had a tea for those on the White House Social Register and it was like old times again, for we were having 793 guests. In preparation for the affair I ordered the pastry section to make lacy roll cookies. Behold—we found that the oven was not yet perfectly even. These cookies are very delicate. The batter is thin and must spread evenly during the baking, for while the cookies are warm you roll them on the handle of a spoon. When cooled, they are very brittle and transparent-looking and tasty. In the new oven we found that when the batter was spread it would run about an eighth of an inch thick on one side, which prevented them from rolling. Of course we did not have lacy rolls for that tea. Eventually the oven was leveled and we had the old ship in shape for the many activities ahead.

We had a series of dinners attended by business men, labor and political leaders who were trying to induce President Truman to run for a second full term. He refused to commit himself. When the insisting grew strong he would always break it off by suggesting a tour of the newly renovated White House.

There was one of these stag dinners on June 24 and, as usual, when the talk began about the President's running again he suggested a tour of the White House. But at this dinner he said he desired to walk out of the White House instead of being carried out. It was then that I felt sure that the President had no intention of running again.

Not too long afterward at a Democratic banquet in the Mayflower Hotel he told the TV and radio audiences of his intentions. Mrs. Truman was very happy over the President's decision.

Then came the Democratic convention and the President sponsored Adlai Stevenson, governor of Illinois, for the top spot. The convention nominated

Governor Stevenson, with Senator Sparkman of Alabama in the second spot. The Republicans nominated General Eisenhower and Nixon, and again the parade of campaign orators swept over the country.

The President invited both candidates to a luncheon at the White House for the purpose of briefing them on world conditions. The Republican candidate refused the invitation but, most naturally, the Democratic candidate accepted. Mrs. Truman and the rest of the family were in Independence for the summer, so that morning when Mr. Stevenson was expected, I went over the menus with the President. He told me that he wanted me to meet the Democratic candidate. This was indeed a courtesy never before extended to a man in my position.

So after the luncheon the President took the governor and Senator Sparkman on a tour of the place. The group went into the ushers' office and he introduced them to the ushers: Mr. Crim, Mr. Searls, Mr. Claunch and Mr. West. I was in the dining room watching the boys break down the table when the President called me.

He said, "Come in, Fields. I want you to meet the next President."

So I went into the ushers' office. The President introduced me, saying, "Governor, I want you to meet just about the best man in this business. This is Fields. He takes care of the food end of the house."

Whereupon the governor said, "By all means, this is the man to know," and he came over to shake my hand. I was fascinated with the warmth of his handshake and his friendly eyes which made you feel at ease. Senator Sparkman I had known for some time.

Next day when the President had finished his breakfast, as usual I presented him the menu for the day. He said, "Fields, you made a hit with my boy, Stevenson."

I thanked him for the courtesy he had extended me by this introduction. The President was sure of the governor's election, for it was the opinion of many of the politicians that General Eisenhower's campaign was bogged down in a dry creek through August and September.

After that the campaign waxed warm and then cold. The climax was Eisenhower's declaration that he would go to Korea himself, if elected, and see what could be done to end the war. The President was making speeches, too, and taking an active part in the campaign.

Mrs. Truman returned early in September and we had a few important teas. One was for the Daughters of the Confederacy. At this particular tea we served a confetti bread. One lady spoke to Mrs. Helm about how good it was and wanted to know what it was called. Mrs. Helm referred her to me, so the lady approached and told me she was from Georgia and wanted to know the name of the tea bread we were serving.

I told her it was confetti bread. She must have thought I said "Confederate" bread, for she said, "I think it is just grand to serve it to this group. It is just too thoughtful of Mrs. Truman and I am going to write her for the recipe."

I never heard if she did or not. Then she whispered to me, "I'll bet you have never served a party like this here."

I replied, "Why, madam?"

"Because," she said, "there isn't a damn Yankee in the crowd."

On October 31 Mrs. Truman left to join the President, who was campaigning and would wind up the trip by continuing to Independence to vote.

Well, on November 4 Eisenhower was elected by a landslide, carrying 39 states. There were two happy people in my family—my wife and my father out in Indiana. Dad said he was beginning to think he would never see another Republican President, and I had promised my wife that if a Republican was elected I would try for a transfer to Boston so she could have a home near the Lahey Clinic.

On November 5 the President, Mrs. Truman and Miss Margaret returned to Washington. When I saw the President I inquired how he was feeling. He laughed, saying, "I feel fine, but you know, Fields, I could have felt a lot better."

Early in December, Mrs. Truman's mother, Mrs. Wallace, passed away. She had been sick for the past year or more. Mrs. Wallace was a kind and lovely person, never complaining through all her illness. She was ninety years old, and though her death had been more or less expected, we were all upset over her passing. The President rushed over from the office, forsaking matters of state to comfort Mrs. Truman the way any other husband would do.

My wife had not been able to return from Boston and the doctors had given her not more than from six to nine months to live. I had talked with Dr. Poppin of the clinic and it was felt she should have home comforts near the clinic. When my first chance came I spoke to the President about transferring to a Federal position in Boston. He said that he would look into the matter, but I would have to stay until the new people got organized.

We had a farewell dinner, a stag affair, for the President's official family, past and present, on December 18. There were many speeches made in compliment to them—even to those he had fired.

Chapter 19

FAREWELL TO THE WHITE HOUSE

A WEEK later the family had their last Christmas dinner in the White House. Miss Mary Truman, the President's sister, was present and Mrs. Truman's three brothers, their wives and Mr. Fred's children were all there. When dinnertime came we had thirteen at the table. The Trumans had no superstitions about the number thirteen, but neither the Roosevelts nor the Hoovers would sit at a table for that number.

Well, we rolled along into January, 1953, and the day of the inaugural was soon—much too soon—at hand. We had been hearing rumors, as there always are, about the incoming family. It is funny how these start, but once started, they never seem to stop. There were stories from the War Department about the temper of General Eisenhower and his ability to blast you with the language of a sergeant.

Mrs. Eisenhower, too, was reputed to have a temper and to be very difficult to deal with. In all my years in the old place, I had found out that people like to gossip. There is no excitement in talking about the good qualities of people, so what you hear is the opposite. Mrs. Eisenhower visited the White House, according to the custom of incoming First Ladies, but she made no tour with Mrs. Truman to meet the help. Mrs. Truman, however, told me she had talked with Mrs. Eisenhower about my desire to transfer because of my wife's health. She had told Mrs. Eisenhower that she was sure Charles Ficklin, whom I had groomed to take over, would make an excellent man to take my place. I thanked her for this.

The President had me go to Boston for interviews about the job transfer. I had appointments with the General Services Administration and the navy yard. First I went to the GSA office and talked with Mr. Paul Healy, assistant to the director, and Mr. Hannon, the personnel director. Mr. Healy made an appointment for me to see the regional director, Mr. J. J. O'Connor.

Upon my arrival at the navy yard Captain Gold, the commander, told me that he would like me to read the job description prepared for me. I read the description and, not being too familiar with the buildup sometimes read into these job descriptions, I almost jumped out of my skin. I was to head two divisions for the purchasing of electronic equipment and submarine equipment— not knowing the first thing about either, plus the fact that my chiefs and sub-chiefs would be men with fifteen to twenty years of experience in their lines.

I told the captain that I would not make my decision until I had had further talks with the GSA people. When I returned there and met Mr. O'Connor, he said he thought they could teach me to be an inspector of general supplies. I accepted this.

When I returned to Washington and told the President about my decision he said, "Oh, you could have learned to handle that job in the Navy all right. But perhaps this is the wisest thing. If you think this is it, we will set it up for you."

We still had received no information about the inaugural plans from Mrs. Eisenhower. The President and Mrs. Truman held a reception to say good-by to the office force and the household. Two or three days before the inaugural we were told that there would not be anything doing at the White House except for the family dinner that night. This was something new, for the old house had always before been a beehive of activity at such a time.

On the morning of the inaugural some of the Cabinet members came in after breakfast to say good-by to the President. Talk was going around about the rebellion of the President-elect against wearing a high hat and President Truman said he would not wear one either.

My crew had all gathered in the state dining room where we said our final good-by to the Trumans. Then the cars pulled out of the ground, and still no information from the Eisenhowers except that there would, perhaps, be trays for dinner.

The old White House seemed so quiet. We had thought that, after not being there for twenty years, the Republicans would want to celebrate, but this was denied the rank and file. After we had listened to the President's acceptance speech the chief usher called my office and told me that Mrs. Eisenhower wanted tea at 4:30 for 200 or 300 people.

"Can you do it?" he asked.

I said, "As far as food is concerned, we can serve two or three thousand. The menus are ready. All we have to do is prepare the sandwiches, and the kitchen and pantry can easily do that.

By 4:30 we had set up for 300 people in the State Dining Room when Mrs. Eisenhower sent orders from the reviewing stand to have sandwiches and 50 cups of tea and coffee sent out to the stand.

Then at 5 P.M. we were told there would be only about 50 people for tea after the parade. So we cut the table down and at 6 P.M. the President and Mrs. Eisenhower, Vice-President and Mrs. Nixon and fewer than 20 others arrived for tea. They did not stay long or eat much, for the dinner hour was near and a dance was to follow. But everything was going along fine until Mr.

Nixon said to Mrs. Eisenhower, "What are you going to do with all this food that is left?"

Mrs. Eisenhower turned and looked at the table. Like so many critics, the Vice-President did not know the story behind the scene and I thought, "Of all things—for a man to bring up a question like this!" Well, I knew then that Mr. Nixon was going to have to grow up, for there would be bigger and more important things for him to do than to watch the leavings from a tea party.

Again Mrs. Eisenhower turned and looked my way. I said, "On occasions when indefinite numbers have fluctuated, we have sent the leftovers to the children's hospitals and homes."

This was my first impression of Mr. Nixon as Vice President and I wanted to put an apron on him. But I was impressed by the President on that initial day. He told a colonel to be sure and see about the status of Mooney, his valet, right away. I am always touched by a man who is interested in the welfare of the people who serve him.

The transformation in the household from one Administration to another is as sudden as death. By that I mean it leaves you with a mysterious emptiness. In the morning you serve breakfast to a family with whom you have spent years. At noon that family is gone out of your life and here are new faces, new dispositions, and new likes and dislikes. You have to learn a new routine and to assure the new family that you are responsible and trustworthy.

The next day, naturally, there was a lot of unpacking. The President had set up the small Blue Room which had been used by Mrs. Roosevelt and Mrs. Truman as their private offices as his art room. He was working on a portrait of Bobby Jones.

From May until January the White House had worn its new coat of renovation, but to get two people to agree on a color scheme, especially women in a home, is too much to hope for. One of the first acts of the new First Lady was to change some of the colors on the second floor, the presidential living quarters. The Fine Arts Commission of the District of Columbia has control over changes in the official part of the house. Otherwise, it would doubtless lose its distinction.

I understand that when Theodore Roosevelt was President the State Dining Room was a hideous sight —more or less like a game room in a club with trophies of stuffed animal heads, shot by the President, hanging on the walls. I have heard Mrs. Eleanor Roosevelt talk about the days of "Uncle Ted" and how awful it was to be enjoying a meal and then suddenly look up to find the eyes of a stuffed moose or some other animal staring down at you.

The new house communication system was supposed to be the latest and most efficient, but this did not meet the approval of the new First Family, so electricians set to work tearing into the walls to set up a system to their liking.

President Eisenhower went into action much like President Franklin D. Roosevelt when he was determined to correct problems created by a long period of Republican domination. However, President Eisenhower was not faced with a domestic crisis as President Roosevelt had been. The conferences the President was holding nearly every morning at breakfast with Secretary Dulles and Mr. Stassen led me to believe that he thought foreign affairs were most urgent. Mr. Stassen's position was not clear to me, but most of the time he was present.

During the time I was with the Eisenhowers there were no family breakfast gatherings. The President never lunched at his desk in the office as President Truman did. He had lunch with the First Lady, served anywhere from one o'clock to two. Of course this was at the beginning of the Administration and no doubt things settled down to a routine later. Trays were the custom for the family dinner and with TV paneled in the walls, it did make watching TV and eating from a tray very enjoyable. The Eisenhowers seemed to enjoy TV. Steaks and a standing roast of beef were their favorite meat dishes.

One day the President gave the crew an unexpected problem. The chief usher, Mr. Crim, was told to get some yoghurt, and the housekeeper and Charles, like Mr. Crim, did not know what yoghurt was. This little incident nearly prevented my transfer being O.K.'d. Charles, whom I had been grooming for the job, had been declining it. Finally Charles accepted, telling Mr. Crim he would do his best, but not to expect him to be another Fields with all the answers. Well, this was flattering, but I have always had the habit when compliments were passed around to sort of take stock of myself. And it made me more or less ashamed, for I knew that I had not always had the answers, but the confidence others placed in me made me search for the answers and never let down people who believed in me.

It was not long before my transfer was effected, and the day came for me to say good-by to the old place. Mr. Crim told me that the President and Mrs. Eisenhower wanted to say good-by to me.

They were in the West Hall and Mr. Searls came for me and ushered me in as he would a person for any other appointment. Both the President and Mrs. Eisenhower have that gift of being able to put one at ease. The President talked about my new job and my Civil Service status. He was very precise about it and said, "If anything goes wrong, let me know right away."

Mrs. Eisenhower was interested in my wife's health. She said, "We appreciate your desire not to leave us, but we all have to do so many things for the sake of our families."

I replied, with a lump in my throat, "Good-by and thank you very much."

It was then I thought that, after all these years, I was really leaving the White House. I walked out the gate on Pennsylvania Avenue, shaking hands with the officer on duty. Then I crossed over the street to the park where I waited for my bus.

As I stood there I looked at the old house, all lighted up, and thought of the many exciting occasions in which it had been my honor and pleasure to have a part. I have often thought how, when we are a part of something, we do find fault and complain and say, "I sure will be happy when the day comes that I can walk out of this place." But, comes the day, somehow it is not always a day of rejoicing. I knew I would soon miss all the responsibilities I so often had complained about.

Within three days I was working on my new job, trying to find something important about counting the numbers of turns of wire on the neck of a broom or the ply of an illustrating board. Testing the strength of a sheet of paper and counting the threads in the warp of a piece of cloth were hard to get excited over.

I said to myself, "It must be tough for a President who has had his finger on the pulse of the world suddenly to find that he is just a plain nobody, in a sense, or a has-been champ. Here I am, almost ready to feel sorry for myself, when after all it is the job that is important. So give your best and forget about the glories of what you now think were the great days."

However, I still would think of the fun we used to have amid all the ceremony and formality. For instance, we had code names for the Presidents so that, for security or any other reasons, listeners would not know whom we might be talking about.

President Hoover, because he seldom smiled, we called, "Smiley." President Roosevelt I gave the name of "Charlie Potatoes." Out in Indianapolis there was a corner Greek grocer whose name was Charlie Pertastumas. He was a real diplomat. When people were displeased he could always sell them something else and leave them feeling that he was doing them a favor. I had an uncle who couldn't or wouldn't call him anything but "Charlie Potatoes." Hence we got a lot of fun out of talking about Charlie Potatoes.

President Truman, because of his outspoken manner, we coded as "Billie Spunk." Often when we were talking about some affair we would say, "Wait until Billie Spunk gets there. He will tell them where to get off." I was not with President Eisenhower long enough to give him a code name, but I don't think the boys on the staff continued the practice.

Many people have asked, "Of all the Presidents you served, which one did you like the best?" When they ask this I think of my mother. She would never say that she liked someone. She would always say, "I do understand them so well and I am sure that they equally understand me." So if the question is "Which one of the Presidents did I understand and which one did I think understood me as a person?" I must say that the answer is President Truman. I always felt that he understood me as a man, not as a servant to be tolerated, and that I understood that he expected me to be a man, sincere in my duties and trying to do what is right at all times.

President Roosevelt was genial and warm but he left one feeling, as most aristocrats do, that they really do not understand one. As if to a less fortunate human being, they extend a charitable, human tolerance, but never permit the right to understand them. My brother, who served him as a valet, and the other valets like McDuffie and Prettyman perhaps were able to bridge this gap and to have the feeling of understanding and being understood.

President Hoover was much like Dr. Samuel W. Stratton of M. I. T. He was an intensely human and kind man, very charitable, but I never felt that I understood him or he me. For the short time that I was with President Eisenhower I sensed this feeling of understanding. Perhaps it is rather presumptuous and unbecoming to one of my standing to attempt any appraisal of these great men, but this is my humble impression.

Here is an example of what I mean. When President Truman is in Boston I always go to call on him. I make no appointment. I merely find out what hotel he will be stopping at and his time of arrival and place myself in a position where he might see me. And he always does. He will call out to me amidst all the people he is with, "Hello there, Fields," and make his way to me and shake hands. Then he will say, "Come on up. I want to talk to you." I felt when he first came to Boston that he would expect to see me and would appreciate my sincere desire to see him.

I would not have dared to assume that President Roosevelt would expect to see me anywhere and recognize me in public. Of course it has been so long since I have seen President Hoover that I doubt that he would even remember my name.

Some people have asked if I was ever aware of the attitude of President Truman before he wrote some of his blistering letters, especially the one to the music critic about his remarks concerning Miss Margaret's singing. Truthfully, of all the men I have known, President Truman never seemed to have a problem. I did not know of any attitude of his by his expression of manners, and I first heard of this letter when I read it in the paper. I am sure no one in the household could tell when he was troubled. President Hoover always wore a serious expression, though he had a keen sense of humor and wit. President Roosevelt could change his expression as suddenly as any actor, and so could President Eisenhower. Like all great leaders, they never permitted themselves to show anything but firmness and confidence.

People have also asked about Mr. Harry Hopkins. Was he really the brain behind the scene? Well, of course I would not begin to know that. One thing, though. Mr. Hopkins was a very sick man during most of his stay and he was devoted to the President. As with most sick people, I think you have to understand that they cannot be all smiles, and it is unfair to point to this as a lack of good disposition.

President Roosevelt was one in a thousand. With his difficulty in walking, he seemed to enjoy living and gave me a feeling that he was contented with his lot. So I can say, from my point of view, that Mr. Hopkins was like so many others in our democracy who give their all to a cause when their personal health really should have forced them into retirement.

During the Christmas of 1953 I received from the White House a copy of the portrait painting of Lincoln by the President to complete the cycle of such gifts from the four Presidents I had served, and I am very proud of this possession. It was during this time that I had information of the changes in the relations of the household help and the going back to a longer workday, similar to the old system. It was said that Mrs. Eisenhower insisted on saving the leftovers—even a spoonful of peas, carrots or a lamb chop. These had to be wrapped up and placed in the freezer. Of course I had doubts about this as to quantity—surely she did not save a spoonful of peas.

At the time of President Eisenhower's second inauguration I spent a week in Washington and, like a visiting fireman, spent most of my time at the White House. I was fortunate in seeing the private swearing in of the President in the East Room and it was like being home again. During this trip I saw for myself the improved freezer system with the tiny packages of leftovers. Charles was doing a grand job and had added some improvements that made me wonder why I hadn't thought of them. I also found that, though Mrs. Eisenhower was a hoarder of leftover dabs, she had a great sense of appreciation, for Charles had many personal notes from the First Lady thanking him for his thoughtfulness in serving a special cake or something else pleasing to her. There were personal notes, too, written by little David for a party served him. Such little memos of thank-you are invaluable.

Many times I have been asked about the children and grandchildren in the White House families. President and Mrs. Hoover had two grown sons. Mr. Herbert, Jr., was married and his family lived for a short time in the White House. He was a very fine gentleman but his quiet, studious way made it difficult to approach him. He was very much like his father in that he did not appear to see others. Now Mr. Allan, though he seldom spoke, was very much like his mother. He could and would spot any breach of service, even the way a servant would walk as he approached the table. One waiter had to be transferred to a houseman's job because he sort of rocked or strutted when he walked. It was the man's natural gait, but Mr. Allan did not like his appearance as he walked to the table and that was that.

As for the Roosevelt children and grandchildren, they were without doubt the most individualistic. Mr. James was married, and Mr. Elliott also. Mr. Franklin and Mr. John were in Harvard, so they were not children. But these young men, when they got together, could raise a real roughhouse. One time Mr. Elliott, Mr.

Franklin and Mr. John had such a rough house in the Lincoln Room that during the scuffle Mr. John sustained a fractured ankle and was laid up for weeks.

Mrs. Hoover during her stay had made a search and found the original Monroe furniture and had it brought to the White House. The Monroe sitting room was set up as an informal room for the serving of teas on the second floor. When the Roosevelts moved in the first thing the President said when he saw this room was, "Oh, my Lord! We cannot have this delicate furniture here. Can you imagine what my roughnecks would do to it after one fracas?" So the Monroe furniture was stored away for safekeeping.

I suppose Sistie and Buzzie Dall were the most popular grandchildren during my stay. They were such sweet children and so friendly. They were devoted to their maid and cook, Kattie, who was with them in Tarrytown. After they left the White House to live in Seattle, whenever they visited Washington they would go to Kattie Hollyness's home in northeast Washington for dinner. They were just as excited about this as if they were going to the Mayflower Hotel. Mrs. Boettiger was a most understanding person, and she and Mr. James were the most friendly of the family. Both Sistie and Buzzie had their mother's charm and they were taught to be unspoiled.

With the Trumans, Miss Margaret was an only child and she was a very attractive and charming young lady in college. I do not think any young lady in our time was ever so suddenly thrust into the limelight as Miss Margaret. Although she was an only child, she had not been spoiled. Mrs. Truman is a woman of great character, down-to-earth ideas and wholesome dignity. Miss Margaret was devoted to her mother, father and grandmother. I can still see her walking to the table, escorting her grandmother by the arm, and Mrs. Wallace was so pleased and happy for her attention.

I must say Miss Margaret did disappoint me in one respect, for I had hoped to plan a wedding in the White House. Despite this, if I live to be 150 years old, I shall always remember Miss Margaret.

As for the Eisenhowers, there were only Major Eisenhower and his children and I was not there long enough to get acquainted with them.

This is my story of some of the happenings I have seen, heard, and had a part in during the long years which I spent in the White House, doing my best to help four Presidents and their families to live and work in the making of world history for our God and country and mankind.

Chapter 20

THE FUTURE OF THE WHITE HOUSE

I HAVE seen in the newspapers reports of various discoveries and changes that have been made in the White House since my departure. As to the "discovery," according to newspaper account, by Mrs. Kennedy of a desk made from the Repulse, I am somewhat skeptical. There must be some mix-up here on the part of the reporters. This desk was always known in my time and, since the renovation of the White House by President Truman, a room was deliberately set aside for this piece and others like it. A record was kept of all the furniture in the White House and whenever people know ahead of time where some thing is, they cannot really discover it.

The newspapers have also mentioned that a campaign has begun to catalogue and list all the chinaware in the White House. I don't know what the purpose of such a "campaign" might really be, since we always had records of the entire chinaware in the Presidents' house, and knew precisely to which administration it belonged. We were able, for instance, to speak of and identify finger bowls that belonged to the Adams administration, the Lincoln punch bowls, numerous donations from Washington's time, and various others.

About the changes that have been made, I am not certain from my experience that they strike me as altogether advantageous. I understand that the Kennedys have installed a kitchen and dining room on the second floor. I can appreciate the desire to have this service available in that place. But I should think that it would entail many problems, especially with reference to getting the food there, the disposal of leftovers, and the odors that would undoubtedly fill the presidential bedrooms. After all, the second floor of the White House is not an average businessman's apartment where the President and his family must be carefully secluded from the public or a place in which the first family is cramped for space. It is the home of the first man of the land—our national leader.

It would seem to me that there are several possibilities for satisfying the same need, such as the use of a thermotainer that can be quickly carried from the first floor. Perhaps the White House help prefers the change to the thermotainer since it is much easier for them to work at close range to the actual dining room. But no matter how easy it becomes for the help—and I am always sympathetic to easier work for the help—I feel something is lost. I am thinking now of the fact that taxpayers might complain that expenses might run higher. What I am deeply sorry to read about is the doing away with a certain tradition of service and ceremonial.

I have often thought what the future of the White House might be. It is my belief that the day is coming when a President will find it necessary to live elsewhere in order to have a real home and so that the White House can be reserved for official entertaining and state functions only.

The President's situation right now is that of a servant who has to "live in"—he begins to feel more and more cramped, the "edge" is taken off his home life, and he feels like a prisoner. Under these circumstances, I can well understand why the President and his family today consider a retreat to the second floor. Next year they may move to the third floor. But after that there is no place for them to go except the roof—which will be mighty cold in the winter, even for Washington.

With regard to the new furniture Mrs. Kennedy is said to be acquiring for the White House, it will be in keeping with the traditions of the place and in line with the tastes of President Adams, who was the first President to live there. But if my guess is correct about the future of the White House, then this furniture may not be useful. It is really useless for state functions and must be viewed as a collection of museum pieces. In addition, it makes the place less habitable for the President's family as long as they stay there.

I believe my opinion can be substantiated by the very fact that the White House is an island in the middle of a sea of public buildings. A President can be completely isolated from society, and genuine home life is very difficult at 1600 Pennsylvania Avenue. I wonder if the American people want the President to live an isolated and cramped life in the White House. I can hardly believe it.

In addition, there is the problem of noise. I frequently heard President Roosevelt remark about "the noise the ambulances made the night before," going into or coming out of the emergency hospital right up the block.

In present circumstances, the White House amounts to something not too much better than a beautiful jail, with the President as a sort of warden. It is a shame, I have often thought, that such a wonderful warden cannot free himself—especially since he is such an exalted prisoner.

I know that this observation on the White House will not cause you to worry that no man will seek to get the job in such a beautiful and regal jail. Every four years there will be men in TV debates and traveling the countryside to prove that they and they alone should be incarcerated in the place, so that all of us can remain free and fulfill the American dream.

Appendix 1

GIFT WINES AFTER THE REPEAL

*T*HESE are the punch combinations that always gave me sleepless nights after having served them at a White House party. In my days the White House budget was a very tight one and if a President indulged in heavy entertaining he would be forced to spend his own money. President Hoover always spent his own money, he did not even take home his pay. President Roosevelt wasn't about to do that so I was ordered to use up all gift wines for a spike punch.

There was sherry, sweet, dry and just sherry, sauterne, claret, muscatel, scuppernog, blackberry, concord, apple jack, white wines and Japanese saki. It has been said that East is East and West is West and never the twain shall meet. One thing for sure—I did a lot of stirring and mixing and hoping some poor soul who might take in just a little too much wouldn't blow his top. I worked these recipes days before a party, for it required tasting and more tasting. Even just rolling the mixtures around in your mouth took courage, but my orders were: use up that gift wine. I thought the President's popularity would never wane with the wineries. So when you really hate yourself someday try one of these combinations, and I can assure you that you will be happy to return from outer space.

To serve 30 people.

1

1 quart claret
1 quart sherry
1 quart sauterne
1 quart saki
1 cup of lemon juice
1 cup of sugar (to taste: depends on sweetness of wines)
1 quart club soda

2

1 quart muscatel
1 quart sauterne
1 quart apple jack
1 quart scuppernong
sugar to taste
1 cup lemon juice
1 quart of club soda

3

1 quart blackberry
1 quart claret
1 quart saki
1 quart sherry
lemon juice sugar to taste (blackberry wine is very sweet)
1 quart club soda

4

1 quart concord
1 quart white wine
1 quart apple jack
1 quart scuppernong
lemon juice 1 cup
sugar to taste
1 quart club soda

Don't you wonder why these mixtures did not cause a tragic ending for some poor soul? I could always see the headline "President's party has tragic end. Guests go besmirched after drinking spike punch at the White House. Chief Butler being held for investigation."

Appendix 2

FAVORITE MENUS I PLANNED
FOR THE WHITE HOUSE

DINNER FOR THE DUKE OF KENT

Monday
August 25
1941

Little Neck Clams

Clear Soup with Sherry
Fairy Toast
Celery   Olives

Roast Turkey
Deerfoot Sausage
Cranberry Jelly   Chestnut Dressing
Rolls
Beans   Cauliflower
Candied Sweet Potatoes

Grapefruit & Avocado Salad
Cheese Straws

Ice Cream
Angel Food
Coffee

Champagne   Sherry

OFFICIAL LUNCHEON DUKE & DUCHESS OF WINDSOR

Monday
June 1
1942

Fruit Cup
Broiled French Chops
Asparagus   Corn Pudding
French Fried Potatoes
Tomato Sandwich Salad

Strawberry Shortcake

Coffee

DINNER

Soup
Steak
Peas   Asparagus
Salad
Apple Pie

THE DUCHESS OF LUXEMBOURG & FAMILY

Tuesday
August 25
1942

LUNCHEON

White Swiss Soup
Olives   Celery

French Chops
Pickled Bing Cherries
Peas   Spanish Rice

Creamed Spinach Seasoned with Onion

Avocado & Orange Salad

Ice Cream
Crushed Raspberries
Gold & Silver Loaf Cake
Coffee

AFTER THEATER SUPPER
FOR CAST OF "THIS IS THE ARMY"

Saturday
October 10
1942

Hot Tomato Soup

Chicken Salad
Cloverleaf Rolls

Celery   Olives   Radishes

Quartered Tomatoes

Ice Cream
Cake
Coffee

LUNCHEON FOR
MARY PICKFORD & DOROTHY DUCAS
INFANTILE PARALYSIS FOUNDATION

Saturday
Jan. 15
1944

Vegetable Consommé

Salmi of Duck
Kumquot Compote

Harvard Beets
Brussels Sprouts
Mashed Sweet Potato Cones
(flavored with nutmeg)

Hearts of Lettuce
Herb Dressing

Cheese and Crackers

Mary Anns
Jelly
Thin Custard Sauce
Coffee

BUFFET SUPPER
GENERAL EISENHOWER

Monday
June 18
1945

Madrilene

Assorted Olives   Curled Celery

Roast Turkey
Dressing
Succotash
Harvard Beets
Casserole Sweet Potatoes

Molded Fruit Salad

Chocolate Ice Cream
Angel Food Cake
Coffee

DINNER FOR HIS EXCELLENCY JAWAHARLAL NEHRU, THE PRIME MINISTER OF INDIA

Tuesday
October 11
1949   *16 @ 8:00 P.M.*

Soup Julienne
Bread Sticks
Assorted Olives   Celery Hearts

Panned Fillet of Sole
Tyrolienne Sauce Sliced Cucumbers
Brown & White Sandwiches

Roast Turkey
Oyster Dressing
Brown Gravy   Cranberry Sauce
French String Beans
Buttered Beets
Casserole of Squash

Gingerale & Peach Salad
Shredded Lettuce
French Dressing
Toasted Triscuits

Vanilla Ice Cream & Orange Ice Molds
Angel Food Cake

Nuts   Candy   Demi-Tasse   Liqueurs

MRS. MESTA

Dinner Rolls

Cocktails:
Old Fashioneds
Martinis
Orange Juice

DINNER

Oysters on Half Shell
Crackers

Sherry Calves   Head Soup
Hearts of Celery   Fairy Toast   Assorted Olives

Fried Red Snapper
White Wine   Black Butter Sauce
Parsleyed Potato Balls

Broiled Breast of Guinea Chicken
on Prune Dressing
Champagne   Wild Beach Plum Jelly
Baked Stuffed Tomatoes & Mushrooms
Casserole of Sweet Potatoes with
Marshmallow
Harvard Beets
Rolls

Green Salad with Hearts of Palms
Wine Dressing (French)
Toasted Triscuits

Macaroon Ring Molds
Brandied Peach & Coconut Cake
Nuts Candies Demi-Tasse Liqueurs

THE PRESIDENT OF FRANCE

Thursday
March 29
1951

BREAKFAST

Fruits	*Juices*	*Cereals*
Strawberries	Orange	Oatmeal
Sliced Bananas	Grapefruit	Cornflakes
Sliced Oranges	Tomato	Cream of Wheat

Poached Eggs on Toast   Smoked Ham
Fried Eggs   Bacon
Scrambled Eggs   Sausages
Boiled Eggs
Egg Omelet

Pancakes & Sausages or Bacon
French Toast, Bacon or Sausages
Waffles, Bacon or Sausages
Melted Butter & Maple Syrup with
all Pancakes & Waffle dishes

Jams

Strawberry   Raspberry   Marmalade   Blackberry

Toast	Muffins	Biscuits	Sweet Buns
Tea	Coffee	Milk	Hot Chocolate

H. R. H. PRINCESS ELIZABETH OF ENGLAND

Thursday
November 1
1951

LUNCHEON

Cocktails:
Old Fashioneds
Martinis
Orange Juice
Tomato Juice
Canapés

Honeydew Melon
Seminole

Smothered Pheasant
Currant Jelly
Bread Sauce
Fried Samp
Broccoli with Lemon Drawn Butter
Baked Stuffed Tomatoes
Rolls

Sparkling
Burgundy

Green Salad Roquefort Cheese Bowl
Radish Garnish
French Dressing
Toasted Triscuits

Stanley Cream Molds
Sponge Drops

Nuts   Fruits   Candies   Demi-Tasse
Cigars   Cigarettes   Liqueurs

DINNER FOR PRECONVENTION PLANNINGS
Tuesday
June 10
1952

STAG DINNER

Cocktails:
Old Fashioneds
Martinis
Tomato Juice
Orange Juice
Canapés

Shrimp Cocktails

Black Bean Soup
Celery Hearts   Assorted Olives
Lemon & Egg Slices
Corn Sticks

Baked Madeira Ham
Raisin Sauce
Fried Apple Rings
Spinach Goldenrod
Candied Sweet Potatoes
Rolls

Hearts of Lettuce
Roquefort Cheese Dressing
Toasted Triscuits

Raspberry Sherbert & Vanilla Ice Cream
Melon Molds
Sponge Cup Cakes
Nuts   Candies   Demi-Tasse   Liqueurs
Cigars   Cigarettes

KING OF IRAQ

Saturday
Aug. 16
1952

LUNCHEON

Cocktails:
Old Fashioneds
Martinis
Orange Juice
Tomato
Juice Canapés

Honey Dew Melon
Lemon & Lime Wedges

Champagne
(If guests are non-alcoholic,
White Grape Juice for them)

Broiled French Lamb
Chops Minted Pears
Shoestring Potatoes
Spinach Goldenrod
Buttered Beets
Rolls

Tomato Aspic Ring
Parsleyed Cream Cheese Balls
Herb Dressing
Wheat Wafers

Strawberry Ice Cream Ring Mold
With Orange Sherbert
Sponge Cup Cakes

Nuts   Candies   Demi-Tasse
Cigars   Cigarettes

LA SENORA. MARIA DEL G.A. DE ODRIA OF PERU

Tuesday
Oct. 21
1952

LUNCHEON

Cocktails:
Daiquiris
Martinis
Orange Juice
Tomato Juice
Canapés

Persian Melon
Lime & Lemon Wedges

Stuffed Sweetbreads
Sauce de la Real
Guava Jelly

Shoestring Potatoes
Buttered Stringbeans
Candied Carrots
Rolls

Stuffed Endives & Cress Salad
Herb Dressing
Wheat Wafers

Sponge Cake Ring with Ice Cream
Snowballs
Chocolate Fudge Sauce

Nuts   Candies   Demi-Tasse
Cigarettes

Made in the USA
Monee, IL
12 February 2023

27603517R00115